The Church That Christ Built

Examining the Framework

2nd edition

Kevin D. Starr

Table of Contents

Preface

In this book, we are about to embark on a journey that will uncover the **Church that Christ Built**. Before we get started, let me give you a little background concerning why this book was put together and what you can expect to read.

I work as an engineer and have 5 generations of church roots in my blood. As an engineer, my work has taken me all over the world. During these business trips, I try to find a place of worship whenever possible. I find that going to church regularly keeps me focused, helps break up the week, keeps me spiritually grounded, allows me to meet wonderful Christian people, and helps bring the genius of our Lord and Savior into focus. In many ways, this book is a marriage of my experience with Bible study and analytical study.

In my work, I analyze data and put the results in a format that allows customers to "see" their process in a different light: I let the data talk. On one business trip, as I was pouring over thousands of pieces of data, a coworker asked if I had seen the movie, "A Beautiful Mind." In that movie, the lead actor is looking for a pattern in a wall of numbers. My coworker told me I reminded him of that scene. Since then, many have asked me if the data talks to me, and in a sense the data does. A few years ago I found one of those "find the perfect job" web sites. I plugged in the requested information and then hit submit. The computer thought for a while, then told me that my perfect job would be a "Data Analyzer." I almost fell out of my chair. Since then I have spent many hours mining data in the hopes of finding nuggets of gold. In this book we will look at Biblical data instead of numerical data, and our goal will be to uncover the **Church that Christ Built**.

Something's in the air?

I have noticed a problem related to finding and defining **the Church that Christ Built**. Take a look at nearly every medium from gospel preachers, Christian songs, emails, television, Internet, and even the latest Christian books. In nearly all of these mediums, it does not take long to hear comments or questions related to **the Church that Christ Built**. For example:

- "We are all part of the body of Christ. It doesn't matter what denomination we are, the point is that we meet at the foot of the cross."
- "We all have different personalities, so to expect us all to attend the same Church is unrealistic."
- "I'm a first generation Christian; I don't see what the big deal is about all the religious rhetoric. I go to this Church because my friends do."
- "I would not attend this religious group if I felt my or my family's salvation was being jeopardized."

- "The fact that there are so many different religious views and churches necessarily imply that there is no single correct answer."
- "I had to look to find a church that accepts my lifestyle as is."

As I hear these comments, I realize they are not that different from comments I hear when I go into a customer's site to help solve a problem. I find it ironic how two or more different groups can look at the same information and come up with such different conclusions. As an engineer, I sort this information out. I have consistently found that the data does not lie. The data is simply misinterpreted. As a result, I wondered if my training could help define what Christ did indeed build. So I asked myself a series of questions:

- Is it possible that the data found in the Bible has been misinterpreted?
- Is it possible that not all of these different views are correct?
- Is it possible that my views may be flawed?

I realized that the answer to all of these questions could be yes. That frightened me and forced me to study. Often, if I don't keep an open mind in the engineering world, my shortcomings can result in hundreds of thousands of lost dollars, hard feelings, and bad days. However, on the spiritual side of the fence, if my views related to Biblical concepts are wrong, then the loss could be more than just a bad day - it could be eternal.

The realization that eternal consequences could be related to Biblical misunderstandings stopped me in my tracks and forced me to remove my religious bias, search for Biblical truths, and allow the Lord to show me **the Church that He Built**. The result is this book.

Mining, Anyone?

I will do my best to present my findings in a logical, Bible-based format with examples, pictures, and references. I have found that once good is defined, recognizing bad becomes much easier. I am reminded of a saying we use in Product Development: If you find you have gone down the wrong path, turn back. There is no value in spending more money to prove you are more wrong. Just stop, learn from the mistake, correct, and improve. This book will arm you with facts so that you can make informed decisions.

Each time these lessons are presented, I find myself more the student than the teacher. I welcome feedback and look forward to growing with you on this incredible journey. I hope you will find this book interesting, informative, and a useful resource, but most of all; I hope it inspires you to find, make, or restore **the Church that Christ Built**. So with that, let's grab our Bible and start digging. Enjoy your journey, the destination is worth it!!!

Chapter 1: Do Boundaries Exist?

Rules, for Them or Against Them?

This may seem like a strange place to start in our quest for finding **the Church that Christ Built**. However, before we start, we need to make sure our thinking is consistent when it comes to boundaries. In many cases we realize there are rules - we just don't like those rules when they apply to us.

Rules, Made to Be Broken?

What is the difference between a goal and a boundary? Could it be that the difference has to do with our perception of the rule? For example, some may see a stop light as a suggestion rather than a restriction.

A few years ago, I was driving in St. Helens, Oregon. I was in a hurry and the light was just turning from green to yellow. I figured I could make it. I did. No one yelled; no horns went off. So I was a little surprised when a police officer pulled me over. He informed me that in Oregon, yellow means stop, and since I went through it, I broke the law. He then went on to give me a ticket and told me to have a nice day. The ticket ended up costing 180 dollars. I am still upset about that. However, those are the rules in Oregon. I looked at the yellow light as a suggestion to stop, not a boundary. Since I broke their rule, I suffered the consequence.

Rules or boundaries can be put in place to protect us. Can you imagine letting your 2-year-old child play in the middle of a busy intersection? Of course you would not do that. However, that 2-year-old may have no idea why you are being so strict. In this example, you happen to know the consequences of playing in the intersection; your 2-year-old does not. Another example that comes to mind is the speed limit. How many people drive 5 mph over, or go with the flow? I am sure there are many such examples.

The problem with rules may have to do with how we view them. Some see a rule as a boundary that should not be crossed or even approached, where others see the same rule as more of a guideline that can be broken if needed. The problem occurs when your view or understanding of the rule is wrong. In either case, there are consequences to breaking a rule.

Have you ever looked at a caged animal? The cage may be huge, but where is the grass worn? Typically the grass is worn right next to the cage. I live near a farm and one time I noticed a cow poking her head through a barbed wire fence. The cow was bent down and straining to get some green grass on the other side of the fence. What struck me as funny was that the grass the cow was trying to eat appeared to be the same height, color, and texture as the grass growing on her side of the fence. I also found this to be ironic.

We need to be careful how we interpret a rule. Sometimes breaking boundaries can be a good thing. In my office, I have a picture of an elephant getting ready to pole vault. The saying on the picture says, "It's only impossible until it's done." When I am faced with what seems to be an impossible request, I look at this picture. Then, if I finish that impossible task, I mentally pat the elephant on the back and say thanks.

Pushing physical and scientific boundaries is what sent a man to the moon, invented airplanes, and developed cell phones. Some boundaries were meant to be broken. We typically call that goal setting. You set a goal, work toward it, achieve it, and then set a new one. That is called progress. Unfortunately, in the game of life, some boundaries need to be respected.

All too often, we act like the 2-year-old or the caged animal when confronted with one of those life boundaries. We see the line drawn in the sand and wonder why we can't cross it instead of looking the other way and seeing all the sand we can play in.

The next section shows a few Biblical examples of people who looked at some of God's rules as suggestions rather than boundaries. They looked at rules as though they were optional, did not apply to them, or were just a suggestion. The results were not very good for these folks. If they had interpreted the rules as a boundary forbidden to cross as opposed to a threshold they could cross, their results would have been much different. In many cases, the rules God put in place seem quite strange to us. Nevertheless, when they broke the rule, they paid a pretty heavy price.

Strange Rules?

God placed several restrictions on the people found in the Old Testament that had to seem strange to them. However, if they did not obey, the consequence could be fatal. Take the following examples of strange rules found in the Old Testament:

Blood on the Ear

I have always been curious with this rule given in Exodus 29, it seems odd.

> Exodus 29:20 –21 [20]Slaughter the other ram, take some of its blood and put it on the lobes of the right ears of Aaron and his sons, on the thumbs of their right hands, and on the big toes of their right feet. Then sprinkle blood against the altar on all sides. [21]And take some of the blood on the altar and some of the anointing oil and sprinkle it on Aaron and his garments and on his sons and their garments. Then he and his sons and their garments will be consecrated.

Then a wise man gave me insight that has turned this from strange to brilliant. He told me it could mean that these men were to dedicate everything they say, do, or go to be in accordance with God's covenant. Whether these men knew the actual meaning is not the point. The point is they obeyed. I wonder if this rule where in place today, would we do it? Or would we figure out a way to change the rule. Would we get a red sharpie and put a small dot on those three places, or go the other extreme and cover half our bodies in red to make sure the spots were all covered? Sometimes we make it difficult to do what God says.

Don't Touch!
2 Samuel 6:6-7 [6] When they came to the threshing floor of Nacon, Uzzah reached out and took hold of the ark of God, because the oxen stumbled. [7] The LORD's anger burned against Uzzah because of his irreverent act; therefore God struck him down and he died there beside the ark of God.

In this case, God had set rules related to who was allowed to touch the ark of God during transportation. Uzzah was not one of those on the list. I am sure Uzzah had good intentions. I am sure he figured he would get a pat on the back for keeping the ark from falling. I am sure those around him were shocked when he dropped dead.

Don't Steal

The Israelites tried to capture a small town called Ai, but failed because Achan stole.

Joshua 7 [10] The LORD said to Joshua, "Stand up! What are you doing down on your face? [11] Israel has sinned; **they have violated my covenant**, which I commanded them to keep. They have taken some of the devoted things; they have stolen, they have lied, they have put them with their own possessions. [12] That is why the Israelites cannot stand against their enemies; they turn their backs and run because they have been made liable to destruction. I will not be with you anymore unless you destroy whatever among you is devoted to destruction.

Joshua set out to find the problem. Someone had disobeyed one of God's rules. God had told the Israelites to destroy everything in a particular town. The problem was, Achan had sticky fingers.

[20] Achan replied, "It is true! I have sinned against the LORD, the God of Israel. This is what I have done: [21] When I saw in the plunder a beautiful robe from Babylonia, two hundred shekels of silver and a wedge of gold weighing fifty shekels, **I coveted them and took them**. They are hidden in the ground inside my tent, with the silver underneath."

Achan must have known the rules. Everyone else in Israel got the message. He must have known he disobeyed; he hid the valuables in the floor of his tent. The remainder of Joshua, chapter 7, tells us that his disobedience cost him and his entire family their lives. God made a pretty strong point here: Don't break the rules.

Special Perfume
Exodus 30:22 –25 [22]Then the Lord said to Moses, [23]"Take the following fine spices: 500 Shekels of liquid myrrh, half as much of fragrant cinnamon, 250 shekels of fragrant cane, [24]500 shekels of cassia all according to the sanctuary shekel and a hin of olive oil. [25]Make these into a sacred anointing oil, a fragrant blend, the work of a perfumer. It will be the sacred anointing oil.

Take a look at the details that God told Moses to follow. What do you think would happen if someone tried to make a copy of this? The Bible tells us the answer.

Exodus 30:33 [33]Whoever makes perfume like it and whoever puts it on anyone other than a priest must **be cut off** from his people.

In those days, being cut off from your people was like a death sentence.

Strange Fire
Leviticus 10:1-2 [1]Aaron's sons Nadab and Abihu took their censers, put fire in them and added incense; and they offered unauthorized fire before the LORD, contrary to his command. [2] So fire came out from the presence of the LORD and consumed them, and they died before the LORD.

In this example, these servants were in charge of keeping the fire going. They must have lost track of the fire and it went out. Getting the correct fire must have been quite an ordeal. So instead of making a fire the correct way, they decided to use their censers to feed the fire. I am sure they thought it would be fine. They must have thought "No one saw it go out, so let's quickly get it going." The problem was, they did not follow God's rules concerning this fire. God was watching, and they paid with their lives.

Keep the Faith
God takes His rules seriously and He expects obedience. He rarely tells why he puts these rules in place, but in the following message to a King we get an idea.

Deuteronomy 17:19-20 [19]The Law is to be with him, and he is to read it all the days of his life so that he may learn to revere the Lord his God and follow carefully all the words of this law and these decrees [20]and not consider himself better than his brothers and turn from the law to the right or to the left. Then he and his descendants will reign a long time over his kingdom in Israel.

The law was to be studied so he would learn to revere (hold in high regard) the Lord. The law was designed to keep one from thinking more highly of himself than he ought, and finally, if he followed the law, the king's descendants would reign for a long time.

What I see when I look at these strange rules is this: We don't have to know why God tells us to stay out of the intersection - we just have to do it. Who are we to question God's authority? Who are we to say that God really did not mean what He said? Again, I am reminded of my kids when they were small. They would stand up in defiance against some of our rules. God must look at us in much the same way. Actually, we get a glimpse of God's frustration with us in the following passage:

> Psalm 81:11-14 [11]But my people would not listen to me; Israel would not submit to me. [12]So I gave them over to their stubborn hearts to follow their own devices.
> [13]"If my people would but listen to me, if Israel would follow my ways, [14]how quickly would I subdue their enemies and turn my hand against their foes!

Can you hear the hurt in our Lord's voice? Can you feel His frustration? I think I can every time one of my children does something I have instructed them not to do. For example, why did you touch the stove when I told you not to? Why did you jump off the back deck with a garbage bag as a parachute when I told you not to? Why did you ride your bike off the retaining wall when I told you not to? Why, Why, Why???

The Lord loves us and wants us to be with Him forever. He built a framework that defines His Church. Our job is to examine this framework, understand the guidelines, and then do our best to follow them. Christ's guidelines do not constrict, they liberate. Knowing what we are not supposed to do opens the door to what we can do.

Stake Your Claim!
When someone comes up with a new idea, they usually try to protect that idea with a patent. A patent is a legal way to make sure no one can use your idea without permission. In my work as an engineer, I have had the opportunity to work on a few patents. The patent process is interesting, and it is very similar to the instructions found in Scripture as they relate to the **Church that Christ**

Built. In order to investigate these similarities, we first need to understand the basics of the patent process.

Patent Process

The patent is made up of three parts:
- A description of the invention.
- A working embodiment or example of what you came up with.
- The claims or intellectual and physical boundaries of the invention.

As the process was described to me, the settling of the Wild West was used. When the West was settled, an individual would "Stake his claim" to a piece of property. The claim or deed would define hard limits such as a fence row, a stream, a big rock, and other references that were not likely to move. These boundaries became the claims of the deed. A landowner could use the claims to keep people off of the property, make sure someone did not start to build on their property and so on. Even today, we understand that property has boundaries and the Bible makes reference to them as well.

> Deuteronomy 27 [17] "Cursed is the man who moves his neighbor's boundary stone."

A patent is a way for an inventor to define the boundaries of his intellectual property. In other words, a patent defines an area in which the invention is allowed to work. As long as the invention works in that area, the rights to the invention belong to the inventor. The patent protects the inventor and keeps other inventions from infringing or using portions of the invention without permission. Inventing something that overlaps another patent is similar to a neighbor deciding to build a barn in your back yard. That would be an infringement.

The problem with intellectual property is that there usually are no physical boundaries. So the inventor has to build boundaries with words that define the absolute area in which the invention is allowed to work. The better the boundaries, the harder it is to infringe on this intellectual area. Two important components of the patent are the body and the claims. The body explains in common terms how the invention works. The claims are written to clearly define the area that the patent works in. The patent protects the invention, stops others from using it without permission, and blocks others from copying it. A patent is even stronger if there is a working embodiment (example) of the patent that shows that the invention actually does work. Once you understand the body, claims, and example of a patent, you understand the boundaries where you are allowed to work.

Church Patent?

Does the Bible act as a patent that defines the **Church that Christ Built**? It dawned on me that we should be able to look at Biblical data to reconstruct the body, claims, and examples pertaining to Christ's church. In this way we can know what we are expected to do from the perspective of worship. In essence, we should be able to reconstruct the fence line that defines the safe haven where God wants us to worship.

For example, can we find claims relating to the following? How often should we worship? When should we worship? Should we worship in a building? How should we praise God? What should we call ourselves? What attitude should we have during worship? Is there a difference between formal and informal worship? Is giving necessary? What is the function of the Church? What is the Church supposed to do? Is there a formal organization for leadership?

These are just a few of the areas (fence lines) that will help define the "boundaries" of Christ's church. Once we identify these cornerstones, we can understand what Christ built and investigate the vast open area that God has given us. Unfortunately, over the course of 2,000 years, men have allowed some of these boundaries to become overgrown, unprotected, unrepaired, and in some cases even moved. As a result, we may very well be reducing the strength and majesty of what Christ Built. We need to go back to the Bible to uncover the patent that defined the original church boundaries. The following figure shows conceptually what we will find.

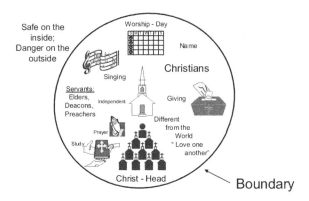

Figure 1: Safe Haven

We will find that Christ describes His Church, with a clear body, a working embodiment, and definite claims. Imagine for a minute how great it would be to have a clear picture of Christ's church. How many arguments could be stopped, how many church splits could be avoided, how many lost souls could be saved? We as Christians could literally change the world. Wow!

Closing Comments
As we conclude this chapter, I wish I could say I understand all of the reasons behind all the things God has asked us to do. However, I can't say that, but I can say that the Creator knows best. As I get older and spend more time in the Bible, some of the reasons behind God's rules are coming into focus. I trust God knows what He is doing. Besides, one day I will have eternity to find out His rationale.

As we proceed, let's try not to focus on why God set boundaries, but rather what those boundaries are and how we make them reality. In so doing we will uncover the brilliant simplicity that governs **the Church that Christ Built**.

Questions to Consider
1. How do you view boundaries versus goals?
2. Do rules make you feel restricted or creative?
3. God was pretty strict in the Old Testament. Do you think He is more lenient today?
4. How have you derived the worship boundaries you currently follow? (Tradition, friendly people, Bible study, etc.)
5. Did Christ start a church franchise?

Chapter 2: Truth

Is There Truth?

Warning Signs

What is the purpose of a warning sign? Signs are designed to alert people to the potential for danger. Each sign is designed for a specific situation. Rarely do you see a warning sign in an area that has no danger. Warning someone about something that will not happen is of no use. I like to tease my kids and often when my daughter is getting ready for a swim meet, I will remind her not to breathe underwater. My point is that if something doesn't matter, why warn someone about the behavior?

Truth Warnings

If truth did not matter, why would God dedicate so many passages to warning us about losing it? Take a look at these few passages related to warnings, and see what conclusion you draw.

- Matthew 7:15 [15]**Watch out** for false prophets.
- Matthew 24:4 [4]Watch out that no one **deceives** you. [5]For many will come in my name, claiming, "I am the Christ", and will deceive many.
- Matthew 24:11 [11]and many false prophets will appear and **deceive** many people.
- 1 Timothy 6:19 [20]Timothy, **guard** what has been entrusted to your care. Turn away from godless chatter and the opposing ideas of what is falsely called knowledge, [21]which some have professed and in so doing have wandered from the faith.
- 2 Corinthians 11: 3-4 [3]But I am afraid that just as Eve was deceived by the serpent's cunning, your minds may somehow be **led astray** from your sincere and pure devotion to Christ. [4]For if someone comes to you and preaches a Jesus other than the Jesus we preached, or if you received a different spirit from the one you received, or a different gospel from the one you accepted, you put up with it easily enough.

Take a look at the highlighted words: watch out, deceive, practice falsehood, do not believe it, guard, and led astray. Regardless of your background, these are strong words for something that "does not matter."

Yes, There Is Truth!

These passages indicate that: Truth is real, Truth does matter, Truth is not out of our grasp, Truth is something we can lose.

How Can Truth Be Lost?

Honey, I can't find my glasses. Honey, I lost my ring. Honey, have you seen my wallet? I don't like to admit it, but I tend to say things like that. I always feel so silly when I lose one of these items. I use them every day. In some cases, not having them can either get me in trouble or even break the law. I know these are important items and that I have to have them. Yet, I still (occasionally) misplace them.

If we can misplace something we use every day, does it seem plausible that we could misplace what we once held as truth? In this section we will look at several ways that truth can be lost.

- Can we forget?
- Can we be tricked?
- Can we be truly sincere, yet still wrong?
- Is there noise in the air that keeps us from seeing the truth?
- Could it be we know truth, but just don't like it?
- Possibly we don't know or were not taught?

Let's take a look at each one of these areas.

Can We Forget the Truth?

A young couple decides they want to invite their family over for a special dinner. During the preparation everything was going fine until the new bride took out the ham and a large knife. She cut 2 inches off the end of the ham and threw it away. This surprised the new husband. He did not want to cause a stink, but that ham was not cheap, so he nicely asked his wife why she just did that. She said, "Oh, this is our family secret. We have done this in my family for years." She went on to explain in great detail how her mother showed her that cutting 2 inches off the ham allows the juices to flow more freely when the ham is cooked. The husband said, "OK" and they went on making the meal. The entire family arrived and the meal was a huge success. The mother proudly told her it was obvious that she had cut the 2 inches off the ham, because if she had not, the ham would have never turned out so good. They both marveled at how their little secret could produce such a great tasting ham every time. Still the skeptic, the new husband asked the mother where she learned the secret. The mother proudly said she had learned it from her mother while helping out in the kitchen. Well, at the next large family gathering, the bride's grandmother came for dinner. She was getting older, but she was still a clear thinker. During the day the new husband found himself alone with the grandmother. He kindly asked her about how she had come up with the secret to cooking such a good ham. The grandmother looked at the boy quite puzzled and had no idea what the young man was talking about. The new husband thought she was just a little confused, so he explained that he had heard she used to cut 2 inches off the ham before cooking it to improve the taste. The grandmother, still puzzled, looked at the new husband and said, "The only reason I did it was so it would fit in my small oven." In this story a misunderstanding became the basis for a family tradition.

We must be careful that our views on truth have a stronger foundation than simply tradition.

Can We Be Tricked?

Have you ever been to a costume party? These are a little strange; no one really knows who they are talking with. I am afraid that one of the best at playing the game of deception is Satan himself. Satan is real and he would like nothing more than to lead us down the wrong path. Rarely will Satan drop a fake truth bomb on us. He likes to tease us over time. In fact, he can even disguise himself as one of the good guys. Satan is smarter than we would like to admit; he is a worthy adversary.

2 Corinthians 11:14 Satan himself **masquerades** as an angel of light.

When I was a teen, I was watching a TV show that had some pretty bad language in it. My dad came by and asked if that show was good for me to watch. I told him that I would change the bad word in my head and that I was fine. He then went into his office and pulled out an article from his files describing how Eskimos kill wolves. According to this article, Eskimos fill raw meat with broken glass, sharp metal, and razor blades. Then they put the meat in the snow and ice. The wolves are attracted to the raw meat. They start to eat, but the ice and snow numbs their mouths. As their mouths numb, they cannot feel what is going on inside them. After a while, they bleed to death. After reading this article, I turned off the TV.

Satan is a pro at making wrong look like a great big wonderful mouth-watering juicy steak. Be careful - that steak may be full of glass. Satan is a worthy adversary. An old friend put it best, "It's a battlefield, brother, not a recreation room!!!" Being a Christian can be difficult, but the benefits are everlasting.

Can We Be Truly Sincere, Yet Wrong?

Seems Right to Me, Must Be OK

I am afraid we can be sincerely wrong. The Bible talks about a person who does what "seems right" in the following passage: Proverbs 14:12 There is a way that seems right to a man, but in the end it leads to death.

Valve to Nowhere

On one job, I was helping troubleshoot a problem with a machine. One of the operators told me that whenever this problem happened, he would go change this large valve on a pipe going down into the floor. He said he had done this for years and it always seemed to make the problem go away. Intrigued by this new bit of data, I decided to trace this pipe to see where it went. Tracing pipes is not always that easy, especially in a large industrial plant where pipes can go on forever. I first went into the basement and looked for the pipe. What I found was a pipe that went nowhere. Sometime in the past, the piping configuration had changed. Instead of taking the entire old pipe out, the mill left some of it in place. Can you imagine how difficult it was for the old-time operator to admit that he had been "fixing" a problem with a pipe that went nowhere?

Wrong Diagnosis

I once asked a doctor how often people misdiagnose themselves. He shook his head and told me that he deals with patients on a daily basis who misdiagnose themselves. He regularly talks to patients who, because of something they have read, are sure they have a problem. He will examine them and often find that what they came in for was just a sore muscle. However, in some cases he will discover a serious problem that the patient knew nothing about. These examples have shown that being sincere is not enough. We must also be grounded in truth.

Godless Chatter?

If you ever played baseball, you probably picked up on this reason for getting truth wrong. When a batter gets up to the plate, what is the defense supposed to do? My coaches would say, "Let's hear some chatter." We would then all start with the chant. Why did we do that? Our goal was to get the batter to swing at bad pitches. We were trying to distract the batter and break his concentration.

The following passage gives us another clue as to why truth can get covered up.

> 1 Timothy 6:19 [20]Timothy, guard what has been entrusted to your care. Turn away from *godless chatter* and the opposing ideas of what is falsely called knowledge, [21]Which some have professed and in so doing have wandered from the faith.

The phrase "godless chatter" is the clue. When I hear this term, I am taken back to my baseball days. However, this phrase is not talking about baseball. This phrase is talking about getting people to miss Biblical Truths. Godless chatter comes in many forms. Have you ever heard someone say something like the following?

- "I do it this way because I am a charter member."
- "They always get credit for doing something. I never get credit for anything."
- "No one said "Hi" to me today at church."
- "The preacher's sermon was pretty dry today."
- "The song leader sure messed up that last song."
- "I am too busy to help out this quarter."

- "The seats are too hard."
- "The elders can't make a good decision."
- "This is the way we have always done it."
  and on and on and on . . .

These phrases and many more can all be classified as godless chatter. What good do they do? They produce a cloud of confusion that makes it difficult to see or even tell truth from falsehood. Once the line between true and false has been blurred, we fall back to our experience to determine what is right. The logic that tells us that if something feels right, then it must be right, is seriously flawed.

I Didn't Know That!

Someone once told me you learn something new every day. I am not sure about that, but if we do learn something every day, that means we don't know everything to start with. An aging lumberjack was getting tired of using his axe to cut down trees. He had heard of a new chainsaw device that had dramatically improved tree cutting. So he saved his money, marched into the local chainsaw dealer, and purchased the device. The salesman told him he had bought the best and that if he had any trouble to bring it in for a free check up. The lumberjack took his new chainsaw out in the woods with pride, but after several hours, he had not cut a single tree down. He was furious. The more he tried, the worse the chainsaw did. He finally took the unit back to the local dealer. He was going to give that young salesman a piece of his mind. He marched into the dealership and threw the chainsaw down in front of the salesman. He said, "This is a piece of junk and I demand my money back!" The salesman, shocked, asked the lumberjack to explain the problem to him. The lumberjack told how he worked all day and did not cut down a single tree. The salesman just could not understand. So he took the chainsaw, pulled on the cord, and it started right up. As soon as that chainsaw started, the eyes of the lumberjack got as big as saucers. He jumped back and yelled, "What did you just do?"

I think I first heard that old story from my grandfather. He really got a kick out of telling jokes. Can you imagine that poor lumberjack trying to cut down a tree by using a chainsaw as a saw? This illustrates that training and background can do a lot to influence our truth system. Unfortunately, not knowing what truth is does not make wrong right.

Mental Database

I certainly am not a psychology major, though I did meet my wife in Psych 101, but that is a much different story. Anyway, I have observed that the thinking pattern of our mind is much like the way a computer works. A computer only "knows" what is stored on its hard drive or what it can access from the Internet. Your brain is a little like a search engine. When you ask it something, it starts going through the storage files in your head. Once it finds something that is a close match, it spits it out. The flow looks something like this:

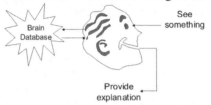

Figure 2: Thinking pattern

Our brain database is populated by our upbringing, training, background, experience, and relationships. For example, if I tell you to think of a red, baseball-sized fruit that has a stem, you will take that phrase, consider all the red fruits you know, and most likely come up with an apple.

It's a Bird, It's a Plane?

Assume you are a frequent flyer. You look up into the sky and you see a plane. You would have no trouble identifying that as a plane. In fact, you may even be able to tell the type of plane based on the way it flies, number of engines, and so on. Next, suppose you are a native of a remote clan that has little or no exposure to the outside world. You are walking through a field with your spear, looking for something to eat. You hear a strange sound and you look up toward the heavens. You see a monster in the sky. Both observers saw the same thing, but their reactions and descriptions would be completely different. The neat thing is that from their perspectives both descriptions would be correct. The problem is, the thing in the air was a plane, not a monster.

The Bible even backs this idea of a mental database. Take a look at this passage.

> Luke 4:45 [45]The good man brings good things out of the good stored up in his heart, and the evil man brings evil things out of the evil stored up in his heart. For out of the overflow of his heart his mouth speaks.

The old adage, "Garbage in, Garbage out" really applies here.

Check the Footers

When buying a house, inspection of the foundation is a must. If the foundation is cracked, then the house is in danger. The same is true of our mental database. If it is cracked, then our truth system is in danger. The problem with a faulty database can be that sincere people come up with very wrong conclusions.

Should have Known Better

Several years ago my boss encouraged me to go back to school to get a Master's in Engineering. I had been a practicing engineer for 14 years, had developed products, received patents, and taught control concepts. I thought that getting an advanced degree would be a snap, so I agreed. Wow, was I wrong! I had a professor tell me I was a good control engineer, but he did not expect me to graduate. I was humbled very quickly by the level of engineering that was being taught. My memory bank was not filled with what it took to get an advanced degree. My mental database was only populated with things I had seen or heard. Boy, were those footers cracked. Fortunately, I did not give up. Instead, I had to strengthen my mental footers by extra study, study groups, tutors, and relearning most of what I had forgotten. Repairing and rebuilding mental footers can be backbreaking work.

Sometimes we need to realize we don't know everything before we can learn anything. We need to look at how we came up with an answer, test our belief system, and make sure our mental database is accurate and up to date. Learning never stops.

Firm Foundation

Some people will say, or at least imply, that there is no truth or absolute, especially when it comes to church matters. I had a person tell me that because there are so many different religions, that fact alone is enough proof that there is no single truth. Some people look for Biblical facts to support their ideas, while others look at people's words to support theirs. Wise counsel is not always a bad idea, but if our mental database does not get back to Biblical facts, we may be building a faith on a cracked foundation. The Lord even tells about what can happen when we take direction from someone with a faulty foundation.

> Luke 6:39 [39]Can a blind man lead a blind man? Will they not both fall into a pit? [40]A student is not above his teacher, but everyone who is fully trained will be like his teacher.

I wanted to make sure I was not blind when talking about Biblical church facts. So I decided to strengthen my Biblical footers related to the **Church that Christ Built**. During my journey, I came across several mental roadblocks that stood in the way of how I worship our Lord. As a result, I began testing my belief system by asking myself "why I believe" rather than "what I believe." One question I asked myself was "Is my mental truth table based on the fact that I am a fifth-generation Christian?" If my foundation is based on this fact, then isn't my belief system based on a tradition? A tradition that is rich in Christian color, but could be no less true than cutting 2 inches off a ham to make it taste better after cooking? I realized I needed to make sure my religious "truths" had a substantial foundation. In order to start that process, I had to not worry so much about "what I believe," but rather "why I believe." The trick I found was to turn the tables on the thinking process. Rather than use our truth database to formulate a response, we need to compare our mental database with a standard to see if what we have in our minds is valid.

This exercise is similar to a story I once heard related to identifying counterfeit money. The story indicated that the best way to teach a clerk to recognize a fake is to spend time teaching them what a real bill looks like. Once the real bill is firmly imprinted in the mind of the clerk, a fake becomes easy to spot.

Comparing our mental truth system against a standard is hard work. The standard when talking about the concept of the **Church that Christ Built** is the Bible itself. The goal of the following exercise is to find out the "why" rather than the "what" in regards to our belief portion of our mental database. The following questions are designed to help you start this exercise of mental evaluation. When looking at the questions, try to evaluate "why you believe" rather than "what you believe".

- Do you attend church service because your parents did?
- Did you hear about church on TV?
- Do you go to worship because your friends do?
- Did you read a book on the subject?
- Do you go for your children or for your spouse?
- Do you go because you like the preacher?
- Do you go to a certain church because your life style was accepted?
- Do you go to a certain church because you have a special talent that your church needs?
- Do you support all the formal church worship services?
- Do you support non-formal church events?
- Can you trace your churches worship activities back to Scripture?

Can you trace your answers to Biblical references? I couldn't, and that told me my mental database had not been well populated. If you find yourself in a similar quandary, the good news is that we can update or mental database by feeding our mind with Biblical truth.

Have you ever tried to drive a car by making corrections to the steering wheel only every 15 or 20 minutes? Of course not! If you did that, you would end up in the ditch or around a tree. When driving a car, you make small changes all the time to make sure you stay in the road. The same is true of our mental truth database. We update our views on Biblical truth by reading the Bible. We have to evaluate our database every day without ceasing to make sure we are headed down the right path.

Recognizing truth may sound pretty easy, but the following passage gives us a hint that trouble is among us.

> Matthew 7:15 [15]**Watch out** for false prophets. They come to you in sheep's clothing, but inwardly they are ferocious wolves. [16]By their fruit you will **recognize them**.

A ferocious wolf in sheep's clothing may sound like Little Red Riding Hood, but the best false teacher can come across as sincere, trustworthy, and even full of knowledge. Sincere people can be dead wrong. Primarily, if we don't keep track of our mental database and make sure it is grounded in the teachings of the Lord, we can sincerely come up with a truth system that is off base and not even realize it.

Tracking Time

Satan is the primary reason that truth and non-truths get mixed up. Consider your activities from the past week: Sleep, work, play with the kids, snuggle with your spouse, eat, work on your hobby, watch TV, go to worship, read the paper, study the Bible, help your neighbor, mow your lawn.

When you take time to look at how thin we are spread, it is no wonder we get distracted. We have a million things pulling at our time. Most people don't set out to head down the wrong path. The trick is to recognize the right path and make corrections to get on it and remain on it.

There is a song that we sometimes sing in worship that has the following phrase from Mathew 6:21 in it. "Where your treasure is, there your heart will be also." We can say our treasure is in Heaven, but the hours we spend during the week can give us away. Time tracking is a great first step toward stopping the bleeding and making sure our truth is in the right place. I encourage you to fill this out for a few weeks. Your grade may surprise you. My grade sure surprised me . . .

We all have 168 hours in a week. If we subtract 8 hours a night for sleep, that leaves us with 112 hours for: God, family, work, self, hobbies, etc. If we apply the principle of paying God first, and use the 10% rule as a starting point, that would leave 11 hours a week for God-related activities. Now, if you want to grade yourself concerning your time with God, take the hours spent with God during a week and plug it into the following equation.

$$\text{Percentage of time with God} = 100 \left(\frac{\text{Actual Time with God}}{11} \right)$$

Once you have your percentage, find your grade. Here is an example:
Time with God during the week:

Grading Scale

Attend Sunday Bible Class – 1 hour

Attend Sunday Service AM & PM – 2 hours

Attend Wednesday Service – 1 hour

Preparation and travel for Church – 3 hours

90 - 100	A
80 – 90	B
70 – 80	C
60 – 70	D
<60	Fail

That adds up to 7 hours for the week, which works out to a 64%. You just got a D for the week. When was the last time you ran home and bragged about getting a D on a test?

Here are some pointers we can use to help improve our grade.
- Attend all church services. (4 to 7 hours per week)
- Find something to do for 30 to 45 minutes every day for Christ. Pray, read the Bible, have a family devotional, talk to friends about Christ, etc. (3.5 to 5 hours per week)
- Support church functions: Fellowships, study groups, outreach. (2 to 4 hours per month)
- Practice random acts of kindness: Visit the sick, send an uplifting card, remember a birthday, take a meal to the needy, etc. (Icing on the cake).

Questions to Consider
1. Evaluate your knowledge bank by estimating your grade based on the time tracking exercise. What goals can you set to increase your grade?
2. If you answer Yes to any of these questions, please provide a Biblical justification to explain your position.
   - Do you attend church service because your parents did?
   - Do you go to worship because your friends do?
   - Did you read a book (other than the Bible) on the subject?
   - Do you go for either your children or your spouse?
   - Do you go because you like the preacher?
   - Do you go to a certain church because your life style was accepted?
   - Do you go to a certain church because you have a special talent that your church needs?
3. If you answer No to any of these questions, please provide a Biblical justification to explain your position.
   - Do you support all the formal church worship services?
   - Do you support non-formal church events?
   - Can you trace your churches worship activities back to Scripture?
4. Read John 10 and ask yourself if you can recognize the Shepherd's voice?

Chapter 3: The Standard

Truth Is Real

Have you ever tried to find someone in any kind of sporting event? When our kids were in the marching band, a parent once said, "You must be so proud." We smiled in agreement. They then asked us where our child was. We smiled and said, "We have no idea." We told the inquiring parent that keeping track of them is like tracking an ant.

The problem is they all look the same in their uniforms. We can track down the section, that is easy, but it is hard to find them in the mix. The reason they are so hard to find is that there are no distinguishing marks that separate them from the others.

God knows that truth can be illusive, so He gives us hints along the way. If we dig just a little deeper, we can actually recognize truth. There are several passages that deal with God's truth. Here are a few:

- Hosea 14:9 The ways of the Lord are right; the righteous **walk in them**, but the rebellious stumble in them.
- 1 John 4:6 [6]We are from God, and whoever **knows God** listens to us; but whoever is not from God does not listen to us. This is how we recognize the *Spirit of truth* and the *spirit of falsehood*.

These passages indicate that truth standards can be found in the word of God. The fruit (works) we produce can tell what standard we strive to follow. The way we live, to whom we listen, how we respond under pressure, and where we get our spiritual information will show if we walk in truth or stumble in the dark.

Improving the Standard?

In order to successfully complete my Master's degree in Engineering, I had to complete a thesis. The thesis grade was based on the content, an oral defense, and structure. My advisor helped me with both the content and the oral defense, but the school provided me with the thesis guidelines. The guidelines were related to how the report should look, type of font to use, line spacing, cover page, layout, etc. I glanced over the guidelines and thought they were outdated. After all, I work in the "real world," had written several technical papers, and had even written a book that had sold over 2,500 copies. I assumed the school would be glad to have me improve their guidelines. Guess what -- I was wrong.

During the final weeks of the quarter when my thesis was being finished, it was time for me to defend it. The defense consisted of a few professors and students drilling me for several minutes on the content. This is a pretty stressful time. After about 30 minutes my advisor and co-advisor asked everyone to leave the room except for me. They told me my research was good, my conclusions were good, and that this body of work would help research in the future. I was feeling pretty good at this point. Then they proceeded to comment on the structure of my thesis. Basically, they tore me apart. In fact, they told me that if I did not change the entire thesis to match the school standard, they would not allow me to graduate. I was dumbfounded to say the least.

Now, I had two choices: Fight them or appease them. My thesis really did look nice. I spent countless hours making it match what I thought a good thesis should look like. When my thesis was compared to my peers', mine was hands down a better looking and easier to read document. However, an old saying came to mind, "The one with the gold wins," so I gave in. Besides, I wanted to graduate. I studied the standards and completely re-wrote my thesis. This took much effort. Once I was done, I had to take my thesis for final approval. I was a nervous wreck by this time. I had made over 30 revisions to the document and hoped I got it all correct. My advisors looked over my thesis and said it looked OK to them, but that the thesis would not be official until the school thesis committee approved it. Now I was really nervous. I took my thesis to the person in charge of the approval committee and handed it to him gently. He did not even read the content. He just pulled out a template guide and placed it on a few pages in my thesis. The thesis committee person looked at me, shook my hand, and said "Good job, you will graduate." Now I was really confused. So I asked him why the rigid standard. He told me the school makes electronic copies of all the graduate thesis reports and that each report had to match the standard so that all the information could be correctly captured. He went on to tell me, "Students spend so much time on their research, and we would hate to lose this information just because we don't store it correctly."

Wow, I sure felt stupid for questioning the standard. I wasted so much time trying to improve a standard that was defined for a purpose. If only I had taken the time to talk to the thesis standard makers first, I would have saved myself much embarrassment and time.

Finding the Truth Standard

In the last example, I was fortunate because all that I lost was some time. However, when looking for Biblical standards related to the **Church that Christ Built**, what could we lose if we try to improve on a standard that was defined for a purpose? We could lose for eternity. Fortunately, we have a standard. In that standard, we are told that there are true worshipers. This implies that there are people who can find the truth standard.

> John 4: 23-24 [23]Yet a time is coming and has now come when the **true worshipers** will worship the Father in spirit and truth, for they are the kind of worshipers the Father seeks. [24]God is spirit, and his worshipers must worship in **spirit** and in **truth**.

This passage indicates that true worshipers do exist. Therefore, they must be doing something right. So we must search out the guidelines or standards they used so that we can identify truth. In this information age, computers change faster than our ability to keep up. The Internet, cell phones, MP3 players, and IPods have changed the way we communicate. Just because you were an expert on an old manual typewriter does not mean you could even get a job today. We are in a world of constant change and constant learning. Change can be exciting for some and downright scary for others.

The nice thing about the Bible is that it has not had any new stories added to it for nearly 2,000 years. The Bible is like a time capsule of truth. We have God's written word. That is awesome!!! The Bible is not outdated and His word never gets old. Digging into Biblical data, not the comments of people, is the best way to identify God's standard for **the Church that Christ Built**.

The best way to firmly imprint Biblical standards in our mind is to practice. We have to practice spending time in the Bible. Anything worth doing takes time, and heaven is worth it.

> 1 Timothy 4:13 "...**devote** yourself to the public reading of Scripture, to preaching and to teaching."

We See Different?

The quest for Biblical truths may take us down some painful roads, especially when we confront people who have different views concerning Biblical standards than we find in the Bible. Unfortunately, these meetings can be difficult, but not always. The way we react and the comments we make can be crucial in defusing difficult situations. In order to help prepare for these potentially uncomfortable confrontations, I have included the following information.

May I Walk in Your Shoes?

Earlier we talked about two very different observers looking at an airplane. Each saw the same thing in the air, but only one correctly defined it. Even though they both think they are right, only one of them is correct. The backgrounds and content of their mental database made the difference between a correct identification or an incorrect one.

The following picture shows how these two observers could come up with different ideas.

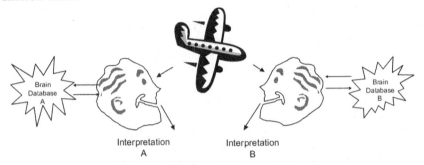

Figure 3: Different Interpretations

In this example, the contents of mental database A and B are very different. Even though both observers see the same item, they provide very different interpretations. Now, suppose that these two observers met each other and tried to convince the other of what they had seen. If this situation is not handled correctly, sparks will surely fly.

How do these two observers work toward a common solution? Guy A could beat Guy B over the head until he changes his mind. This method may be fast, but it does not build very long-lasting relationships. A better option is to get both parties to understand what is in their mental database. In other words, each should strive to view each interpretation from the perspective of the other person. This option takes much more time, but the results can be everlasting. This example is based on two observers looking at an airplane. However, any time you take two people and have them look at any topic, even Biblical ones, the same problem can occur. When people with different backgrounds come up with different interpretations of a Biblical point, there are three possible reasons for the different ideas:

1. Interpretation A and B are both wrong
2. Interpretation A or B is wrong
3. Interpretation A and B are both correct

Given these three assumptions, option 1 or 2 is possible, but option 3 is not possible. Assumption 3 is not possible because there cannot be two different interpretations of a Biblical point. In the case of the airplane, no matter how hard the observer who saw a monster makes his case, what was in the air was a plane, not a monster.

Work Toward a Solution

If we are not careful, our discussion will turn into a confrontation if we corner the other person and try to force him to admit that his mental database is wrong. No one likes to be told they are wrong. Often we can tell when we reach this point when the other person says," Who died and made you judge?" The Bible even warns of such behavior in Mathew 7:1-5. In this passage someone with a large beam stuck in their eye is trying to point out sawdust in someone else's. Let's not first assume we are right. Maybe neither of us is correct, but together we can work toward a solution.

I May Be Wrong?

Working toward a solution tends to deflate confrontation when different views of the same Biblical point arise. If both parties would take a minute to realize that if each had the same background, training, and experience as the other, they both would likely come up with the same interpretation of the same Biblical point. If we can entertain the thought that we could be wrong, then finding common ground can be much easier.

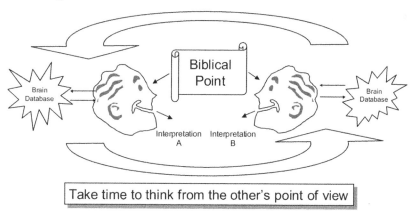

Figure 4: Strive for a solution

On one occasion, I had written a report for a customer concerning their process problems and had provided several solutions. I had backed up my solutions with solid data, submitted the report to the customer, and thought I was done. However, one of the managers read my report and thought I was completely off base. He felt my conclusions were wrong and demanded a meeting. As I was approaching his office, the salesman I was with was trying to coach me on how to handle this guy. Apparently he could be quite difficult at times. When we walked into the room, my report was laying on his desk with red ink all over it. As we introduced ourselves, I thought I detected a Scottish accent. Several years ago, my wife and I and another couple went to Scotland. Before he even started on the report, I asked him what part of Scotland he was from. He stopped in his tracks. He was ready for a fight, not to reminisce about his hometown. However, he could not resist talking about Scotland. He told me the name of his hometown, and it turns out that was one of the towns Kim and I had visited. I shared my memories with him and we must have talked for close to 15 minutes. As we were talking, I realized I knew some engineers who worked in Scotland and asked him if he knew them. This really is a small world, because he did know them. We talked about them for a while and both agreed these fellows were very sharp. I then added that I had trained one of them when they were last in the States. He looked at me and said, "Maybe you can teach me about this report?" We then went through it. I could see the source of his frustration and he could see the reason for my conclusions. When finished he agreed with all my findings. As I left the office, we shook hands, he gave me his business card, and he told me he had enjoyed our talk. The salesman could not believe what had just happened.

There was a little luck in this one, but finding common ground in both Scotland and coworkers was an important step in working toward a solution. If I had gone into that office with the idea that I was right and he was wrong, the outcome would have been much different.

I find that analyzing a problem from the accuser's perspective takes time. However, when I take the time, I can gain great insights into the database in their brain. A great book that gives much more detail on how to do this is Dale Carnegie's book, *How to Win Friends and Influence People.* I don't care for the title, but this book should be required reading for anyone who works with people. When we are working toward a solution, even if we are sure we are right, have patience with those who have views that are different. This Godly advice can be seen in 2 Timothy 4:2. I give you this charge: [2]Preach the Word; be prepared in season and out of season; correct, rebuke and encourage - with **great patience and careful instruction**.

The Bible is filled with truths that can be used to correct, rebuke, and encourage our brothers and sisters. However, the Bible is not to be used as a club. We are to use the Bible with great patience and careful instruction.

Like-Minded
Getting to a common solution is not easy. However, our job should be to work in that direction. God tells us to work toward unity, so this should be our goal. These next passages indicate that God wants us to never stop working toward a solution.
- 1 Corinthians 1:10 [10]I appeal to you, brothers, in the name of our Lord Jesus Christ, that all of you agree with one another so that there may be no divisions among you and that you may be perfectly united in mind and thought.

- Philippians 2:1-2 [1]If you have any encouragement from being united with Christ, if any comfort from his love, if any fellowship with the Spirit, if any tenderness and compassion, [2]then make my joy complete by being **like-minded**, having the same love, being one in spirit and purpose.

Always a Solution?

I wish I could say that things will always work when we: View the problem from the other's perspective, entertain the idea of being wrong, look for common ground to build on, and compare the solution with a valid standard.

The problem is some people refuse to change. Their mental database has become "fact" and they cannot entertain the idea of being wrong. The Bible warns that there will be those who will not listen to sound doctrine.

- 1 Timothy 4:1-2 [1]The spirit clearly says that in later times some will **abandon the faith** and follow **deceiving spirits** and things **taught by demons**. [2]Such teachings come through hypocritical liars, whose *consciences have been seared* as with a hot iron.
- 2 Timothy 4:3-4 [3]For the time will come when men will not put up with **sound doctrine**. Instead, to suit their **own desires**, they will gather around them a great number of teachers to say what their **itching ears** want to hear. [4]They will turn their ears away from the truth and turn aside to myths.

There will be those who will not listen. Let's make sure we are not those people. In fact, the best example illustrating how some have distorted their version of Biblical truth and what we are to do about it can be found in the following verse.

Romans 16:17-18 [17]I urge you, brothers and sisters, to **watch out** for those who cause divisions and put obstacles in your way that are contrary to the teaching you have learned. **Keep away from them.** [18] For such people are not serving our Lord Christ, but their own appetites. By smooth talk and flattery they deceive the minds of naive people.

A friend of mine's philosophy on life is appropriate here. She told me she wanted to be a person of whom others would say the following, "She was trainable." What a great way to live life. We all have something more to learn. Working toward a solution is not always easy, but if we try to understand each other's point of view and check our own mental database against the Biblical standard, then we should both be able to align our mental database with the truth and come up with a common solution. Our goal should be to continually evaluate our mental database. This was also the advice that Paul gave to Timothy in the Scriptures.

1 Timothy 3:14-15 [14]But as for you, continue in what you have learned and have become convinced of, because you know those from whom you learned it, [15]and how from infancy you have **known the holy Scriptures**, which are able to make you wise for salvation through faith in Christ Jesus.

Paul is telling Timothy to have confidence in his mental database. Paul knows that Timothy will have to defend the faith on many occasions and Paul is giving him a little pep talk, letting him know that his truth standard is valid. In order to help make sure we can evaluate our mental database correctly, we need to look at a few ideas on how we can use the Bible as our standard.

Digging for Gold

Have you ever heard anyone say, "I like to weigh myself at home, because my scales read 5 pounds lighter than the scales at the doctor's office"? Or better yet, "I don't weigh myself at all, that way I don't know I'm overweight." Either not measuring or using a faulty scale as the standard results in poor weight management.

If the standard we are using to measure Biblical correctness is faulty or not closely followed, then danger is eminent. When we evaluate our mental truth database, we must be sure that the standard we are using is perfect. Then, when we find a difference between our thinking and the standard, we can be sure the standard is not at fault.

God Breathed

The Bible tells us that the original designer, God, was active in getting His thoughts on paper. Paul tells Timothy that all Scripture is God-breathed.

1 Timothy 3:16-17 [16]All Scripture is **God-breathed** and is useful for teaching, rebuking, correcting and training in righteousness, [17]so that the man of God may be thoroughly equipped for every good work.

Paul goes on to tell Timothy that the Word is useful for teaching, rebuking, correcting, and training. God loves us enough to get His words on paper so we can read His will for us. If the Master of the universe thought His words were important enough to have them put on paper, then I want to hear them, study them, and apply them to my life. My job is not to warp the Word to match my truth database. My job is to change my truth database to match God's words.

No Contradictions

People are always trying to find fault in the Bible. It seems to me that after several thousand years of people trying, someone would have come up with valid and substantial examples of contradictions in the Word. These contradictions have not been found. In fact, whenever someone thinks they found a problem, it is not too long before an archeological dig or scientific discovery will uncover a fact that backs up the Bible's writings.

The amazing fact about the Bible is that it spans time from creation to the 1st century Church. There were several authors all under the direction of God, and there are no contradictions. This little book I am putting together is full of problems. Someone once told me that the book you write will have a finite number of words, but an infinite number of mistakes. That is for sure. However, God's book has no errors or contradictions. Some have said that the book was compiled by a bunch of guys in the 1st or 2nd century. They only included the books that did not contradict each other. I have a problem with this view. Again it seems to me that if the Creator of the universe can keep the earth from smashing into the sun, can keep the stars in the sky, and can create life, then getting His words on paper and making it stand the test of time is not that big of a deal for Him.

All too often, people who come across a point in their mental database that does not match the Biblical standard will start to question the standard. They may comment that the Bible is not really from God, there are missing books, there are contradictions, or that some of the Bible's original intent has been lost as it has passed from generation to generation. They believe that if they can cast doubt on the validity of the Bible, then they can ease their conscience into thinking their mental database is fine. What a dangerous road to travel. We are talking about the Word of God. God did not make any mistakes. His Word has stood the test of time. There are no contradictions, there are no missing books, and the Bible contains all we need to know. If we find that our mental database is different than the standard, we need to fix our thinking, not fix our Bible.

Method of Study

I once heard a funny story about a babysitter. The new babysitter was taking care of a couple's young children. One morning the kids wanted pancakes. The baby sitter did not have a lot of cooking experience, but the kids were persistent. So the babysitter got out the pancake mix, read the directions, and started making the pancakes. In essence, the baby sitter had found the standard for making pancakes and was attempting to make them. Unfortunately, things went wrong. The young kids were trying to help, but for some reason the pancake mix would not stick together. The babysitter called her mother and asked for help. They both went through the recipe and found that all the ingredients were fine. Her mother could not figure out what the young babysitter had done wrong and went over to help out. When she arrived, she immediately found the problem. The young baby sitter had wrongly interpreted the part of the recipe that said to add eggs. She had fried the eggs before adding them to the pancake mix. No wonder those pancakes did not turn out. This is a pretty funny story. However, even the best intentions with the appropriate standard can still be interpreted incorrectly.

Law of Silence

When my son was in preschool, we went to watch a school program. The year before, my son found it humorous to make faces at the audience while on stage. This year I told him that he was not to make the faces he did last year. We went through each face and said that was not to happen again. He said, "OK Daddy" and went on stage with the other students. Well, the program went on a little longer than it should have and my son was getting squirmy. Then I noticed him going through all the faces in his head that he was not allowed to do. He was checking them off in his head. I could almost see the wheels turning and him thinking "I'm not supposed to do this face, that face," etc. Then he stopped and looked at me with a big smile. I was helpless and knew we were in trouble. He proceeded to make a new face, one that we had not seen before. I wanted to crawl under the seat, but in his mind he had not made the same faces he did last year. However, he still did what he wanted. This simple example illustrates one of the problems with the Law of Silence.

Prohibitive or Permissive

During the Reformation Movement in the 1800's, Thomas Campbell said, "We speak where the Bible speaks and remain silent where the Bible is silent." He was trying to get back to the basics. The church had gone in so many different directions that recognizing the **Church that Christ Built** was very difficult. Campbell felt that by only acting on what the Bible said and remaining silent on the areas that were not written would solve the confusion related to following Christ. His idea seemed simple enough, but the example of my son helps show how the law of silence can be manipulated. The crux of the problem has to do with Biblical silence being prohibitive or permissive. If we are on the side of the fence that believes Biblical silence is prohibitive, then we would say, "That which is not written is forbidden." In other words, we would ask, "Where does the Bible say we can do this?" On the other side we would believe that Biblical silence is permissive. In this case we would say, "That which is not written is permitted." On the permissive side of the fence we would ask, "Where does the Bible say we can't do this?" The result of having two sides of a fence is division. One passage in the Bible that helps us see God's side of the fence is found in Jeremiah 7:30-31. In this passage, the Lord is upset. The people were burning their sons and daughters. The Lord is telling them that they had done wrong. In fact, they did things our Lord had no intention of ever asking them to do. In this example forbidden conduct was equal to unauthorized conduct, which was equal to making God mad.

God created the heavens and the earth. He is mightier than our ability to comprehend. When we add to or subtract from His Word, we are letting Him know we know more than He does. God told us what to do and that should be enough.

Silence – A God Thing

We will make mistakes along the way, but if we stick to doing or at least trying to do what God has said, then we are operating in a way that will make our Lord smile. When we try to use God's words to allow us to do what we really want to do, we can get ourselves sideways pretty quick.

Not filling in the silent areas of the Bible with our personal preference is difficult. Many will read this and ask where the Bible says to use electricity, have padded pews, wear shoes to worship, etc. Some will say those who claim to follow the prohibited side of the Law of Silence really are warping the Scriptures in a way not intended by God. These are all valid points, and we will touch on them as we proceed through this book. However, we must not read into areas that God has not given us permission to go. The following passage comes to mind.

> Deuteronomy 29:29 The **secret things** belong to the Lord our God, but the things revealed belong to us and to our children forever, that we may follow all the words of this law.

This passage tells us that the revealed will of God will take us a lifetime to figure out. Why would we waste precious time looking into areas that lead nowhere? When it comes to God and silence, there are a few points that should be made.

- **Silence** is sometimes the unrevealed will of God that a man cannot know and does not need to know.
- **Silence** sometimes pertains to incidentals – the ways and means of doing something that is commanded in the Scriptures, but about which details are not revealed.
- **Silence** is sometimes exclusive. Silence would disallow anything beyond that which is clearly revealed.

Recognizing the brilliance and power of God is the first step in really trying to obey Him. Obedience is the key. We have to strive to do His will. God does know best and He does tell us what we need to know. Applying the written word to our life will take a lifetime to master. Looking for loopholes leads us down the wrong path.

Logic: AND vs. OR

In the world of logic, AND and OR are very powerful tools. A logical AND statement says that something cannot be both true and false, while a logical OR statement allows for something to be true or false. Consider the following:

Assume I tell my son, "I will give you 10 dollars if you clean the garage **AND** wash the car." My son comes in and says, "I washed the car. Can I now have the 10 dollars?" I inform my son that he did not do both tasks. He says, "Come on, I didn't understand. Give me 5 dollars, and let's call it even." What should I do? In this example, my intent was for my son to do both tasks. That is why I used the logical statement AND. Since he only did one task, he should not be given any money. My son changed the AND to an OR. He assumed I would give him money if he did one OR the other task. If I had used the logical OR statement, then his thinking would be right and I would be obliged to give him the 10 dollars.

If we do not appreciate the difference in these logical terms, then we may be misinterpreting important Biblical concepts. For example, if we use an OR statement when actually the Biblical uses an AND statement, then confusion is soon to follow. The result can be sincere people who are wrong.

In the case of my son, I would not have been obligated to give him any money. As a Dad, I would have wanted to give him the money. I am afraid there will be many people in a similar boat when the Lord returns. The Lord has very clear commands in His written word. However, if people sincerely confuse them, then the Lord has to make what many would consider a difficult decision. He, as the Judge, has a very clear answer. Ignorance of the commands is no excuse. Try telling the officer you did not know the speed limit. You will probably still get a ticket. The Lord as our Savior wants us all to be with Him forever. We need to make sure that God's eternal decision for us is an easy one to make. Our mental database and Biblical truths must be in alignment. We must strive to understand what His will is for us as it pertains to the **Church that Christ Built** as well as in all areas of our life.

Mathew 7:21-23 informs us that things don't work out well for those how claim to be Christians, but do not do the will of our Father. Doing as the Lord commands is serious. Eternity depends on it.

CENI
CENI stands for Commands, Examples, and Necessary Inferences. This is a method for ensuring we stay in the context of what God has told us to do.

Commands
The Scriptures contain commands. For example,
- Matthew 22:36-40 [36]"Teacher, which is the greatest commandment in the Law?" [37]Jesus replied: "'Love the Lord your God with all your heart and with all your soul and with all your mind.' [38]**This is the first and greatest commandment**. [39]And the second is like it: '**Love your**

neighbor as yourself.' [40]All the Law and the Prophets hang on these two commandments."

- Deuteronomy 5:32-33 [32]So **be careful** to do what the Lord your God has **commanded** you; **do not turn aside** to the right or to the left. [33]Walk in all the way that the Lord **your God has commanded** you, so that you may live and prosper and prolong your days in the land that you will possess.

The Lord's ways are just as valid and accurate today as they have ever been. The Scriptures contain commands, and we have to find them, interpret them, and live by them.

Examples
Examples often are used to help illustrate how a command is to be carried out. They illustrate and offer insight as to how to act or not act in particular situations.

1 Corinthians 11: 1 Paul said, "Follow my example, as I follow the example of Christ."

Positive examples are intended to comfort, encourage, inspire, and spur us on to love and good works. Looking into Scripture and "seeing" how the early church applied the commands of Christ provides us with tremendous insights as to how these commands are supposed to be implemented. We should always make sure the background to an example has Biblical roots. The world is full of good people who have never opened the Bible. Being a good person does not equate to Biblical accuracy. We must be careful whom we follow.

Mathew 15: 14 If a blind man leads a blind man, both will fall into a pit.

Necessary Inference
The Bible was written in a time and a culture that is foreign to most of us in this age. Determining how the commands and examples can be applied today is a necessary inference. A necessary inference draws conclusions about Biblical concepts that are not specifically stated in the Scriptures. The Bible gives several examples of Christians meeting together for worship.

Acts 20:7 On the first day of the week we came together to break bread.

However, the Bible does not say how they got there. We can see from their example that worship is something Christians do together and the necessary inference related to how we get there really does not matter to God. He just wants us there. Interpretation of the Scriptures necessitates that we make inferences. The problem with the necessary inference is our tendency to go beyond the original intent. We must make sure that the necessary inference can be tracked back through examples to Biblical commandments. Otherwise we may be getting our necessary inference from personal preference.

Closing Comments

Awesome God!!!

Our God is awesome. When you stop and take a look around, you can see His handiwork everywhere. Whether I find Christ's church in a third world country or in the richest countries in the world, it is awesome to see how similar they are. This really should be no surprise. If the same blueprints to a building were given to different builders, their construction would be quite similar when finished. We have the blueprints to the **Church that Christ Built** at our fingertips. We owe it to ourselves to open the Bible, read it, study it, apply it to our lives, and ultimately uncover Christ's church. In 2nd Timothy 2:11-13 we read a trustworthy saying:

If we died with him, we will also live with him;
[12] if we endure, we will also reign with him.
If we disown him, he will also disown us;
[13] if we are faithless, he remains faithful, for he cannot disown himself.

This passage tells us that the responsible for searching out His ways and remaining faithful to Him belongs to us. If we choose not to walk in His ways, He will disown us. The choice is ours.

What is the Key?

Our quest to uncover the **Church that Christ Built** can be confusing. There are so many different ideas about church worship pulling at us. Recognizing the standard can be difficult, but not impossible. The Bible is full of Biblical data or clues related to Christ's church. Our job is to find those clues and compare them with the church we are attending or are going to attend. If the clues don't match the actions of the church we attend, then that church is not following the blueprints that Christ put together.

Questions to Consider
1. What are some of the "secret" things that we try to look into?
2. Why are we so concerned about what God has not told us?
3. What are some examples of how the terms "and" and "or" can be used incorrectly?
4. Pick any activity in the worship of your choice and trace it back to a Biblical command, example, or necessary inference.
5. Where does confusion come from?

Chapter 4: Worship Woes

What is Worship?

Over the years, I have had the opportunity to work for several managers. Some were good and some were terrible. I learned from both. Those managers that were bad, I studied what they did and tried to avoid those practices. Those that were good, I tried to mimic their actions. This is how we are going to start our study of how to worship. Scripture tells us in John that the Father is looking for true worshippers.

> John 4: 23-24 [23]Yet a time is coming and has now come when the true worshipers will worship the Father in **spirit and truth**, for they are the kind of worshipers the Father seeks. [24]God is spirit, and his worshipers must worship in **spirit and in truth**.

The implication being if there are true worshippers, then there must also be false worshipers. In this chapter, we are going to learn how to worship by first removing the wrong ways. Knowing what makes God mad is a big step toward finding what makes God happy. The **Church that Christ Built** is awesome when found, but disappointing when faked. The remainder of this chapter will review several examples of the **Church that Christ Did Not Build**.

Worship Misdirected

A few years ago I took my family with me on a business trip. On Sunday, we started looking for the address of the church we had found in the phone book. As we drove down the street, there were several church buildings and none of them were very well marked. We drove into the parking lot of the address we had and were greeted by the preacher. I asked him if this were the **Church that Christ Built**? He grinned and said proudly, "Is there any other?" I looked up and down the street at the other buildings, but since we were there, we went in. At the time our children were very young and we had given them a toy to occupy their time. Midway through the service one of the kids dropped the toy on the wood floor. Every member turned and looked at us with a look that said, "Keep your kids in order!" My wife and I were amazed and embarrassed by their response. This was not a warm and welcoming congregation to visitors. I recall Jesus scolding his apostles for not letting the little children come to Him. A few years later, my work took me back to that area. I looked for this church and guess what, it was gone.

Misdirected worship either replaces God with other objects or adds God to the list of already worshiped objects. In either case, misdirected worship is worship that misses the mark. The Bible is very clear about what not to worship. The four different types of misdirected worship that will be covered here are: Satan, Angels, Saints, and Idols

Satan

I do not understand how this form of misdirected worship is even possible. However, even today we hear of satanic rituals and Satan worship in the news. We really should not be so quick to look down on people who have fallen into Satan's snare. Satan even once tried to get our Lord to bow down to him. Read Matthew 4:1-11 to see the Biblical account of Satan's failed attempt to get our Lord to worship him. This is an amazing story and one whose purpose I do not fully understand. Maybe God knew Christ needed a test to show He was ready for the road He was about to travel, or maybe God knew Satan needed to be put in his place. Regardless of the reason, I don't doubt this interchange took place.

If we take a closer look at what Satan tried to do, we can get a glimpse into a professional trickster's bag of tricks. First, notice that Satan did not go after Christ when He first went into the desert. No, he waited until our Lord was weak and starving. I can hardly go a day without eating. Can you imagine 40 days without eating? Second, Satan tries to get the Lord to turn some rocks to bread. Imagine how much Christ wanted a piece of good bread. Satan went for the easiest temptation first. However, Christ put Satan in his place by saying that the word of God is enough to live on. Satan does not walk away. He moves into phase two of his deception. He knew Christ was hurting and that getting angels to attend to Him had to sound good. Satan plants a seed by taking Christ to the high point of the temple and telling Him to jump off. Satan assures Him that this act will surely get the angels on their way. However, this trick also failed. Christ told Satan that testing God is not a good idea. Finally, Satan tries for a third trick. He takes Christ up to a high mountain and showed Him wealth and splendor. Satan must have thought that since Christ had been in the desert for 40 days, a good night's rest in a nice place would surely get Him to stumble. Satan made his plea, "Bow down to me, and all this will be yours". I am sure Christ saw through this trick as He did the first two and quickly put Satan in his place. He said that we are to worship only God!!! At this, Satan knew he had been beaten and he left Christ alone. Once Christ had won this battle, God allowed His angels to come to His aid.

What a story! I have to think that the sight of angels flooding out of heaven to come to the aid of Christ would have been something like a baseball player hitting a grand slam homerun in the bottom of the 9th with two outs, two strikes, and down by 3 runs to win the last game of the World Series. The teammates would have cleared the bench and welcomed the slugger with a hero's welcome. I can almost imagine the angels lining the heavenly realms watching this battle take place. Then when Christ won, they must have gone crazy. Of course, we don't know for sure how the angels came to help Christ, but they did. Christ is a hero.

Angels

There have been volumes written about angels and there is much in the Bible about them. In short, angels are heavenly beings who do what God asks them to do. In Hebrews 13:2 the Bible says: Do not forget to entertain strangers, for by so doing some people have entertained angels without knowing it. So, apparently they are still active. There are a few examples of people who came face to face with an angel, and it really shook them up. Take Daniel, for instance. When he saw the angel Gabriel, he fell face down and was terrified.

> Daniel 8:17-18 [17] As Gabriel came near the place where I was standing, I was terrified and fell prostrate. "Son of man," he said to me, "understand that the vision concerns the time of the end."
> [18] While he was speaking to me, I was in a deep sleep, with my face to the ground. Then he touched me and raised me to my feet.

I think this would be my reaction as well. Gabriel must be quite a sight. The Bible tells us he is allowed to stand in the presence of God in Luke 1:19. Can you imagine the power of a being that is allowed to stand in God's presence? Wow, that puts chills up and down my spine. I think if I saw a being like this, my reaction to worship this angel would be similar to John's account in Revelation.

- Revelation 19:10 At this I fell to worship him. But he said to me, "**Do not do it!** I am a fellow servant with you and with your brothers who hold to the testimony of Jesus. **Worship God!**"
- Revelation 22: 8, 9 [8]I, John, am the one who heard and saw these things. And when I had heard and seen them, I fell down to worship at the feet of the angel who had been showing them to me. [9]But he said to me, "**Do not do it!** I am a fellow servant with you and with your brothers the prophets and of all who keep the words of this book. Worship God!"

In both accounts, John dropped down to worship the angel. However, the angel immediately told John not to worship him, but God. Angels do God's work, but they have no authority to allow themselves to be worshiped or to contradict the written word.

> Galatians 1:6-9 [6]I am astonished that you are so quickly deserting the one who called you by the grace of Christ and are turning to a different gospel— [7]which is really no gospel at all. Evidently some people are throwing you into confusion and are trying to pervert the gospel of Christ. [8]But even if we or an **angel from heaven** should preach a gospel other than

the one we preached to you, let him be eternally condemned! [9]As we have already said, so now I say again: If anybody is preaching to you a gospel other than what you accepted, let him be eternally condemned!

Apparently the Colossians were getting a little confused on the concept of whom to worship. Paul warns them in Colossians 2:18 not to worship angels.

Colossians 2:18 [18]**Do not** let anyone who delights in false humility and the **worship of angels** disqualify you for the prize.

Paul says that worshipping angels will disqualify us from the prize. The prize in this case would be Heaven. I can't think of a better reason not to worship angels. One of my favorite passages on angels is 1 Peter 1:10-12. In this passage Peter is talking about our salvation through Christ. Many of us will not believe because we cannot understand why Christ would die for us. We are not alone in our lack of understanding. The end of verse 12 tells us that "Even angels long to look into these things." I find this passage very interesting and reassuring. Even angels don't fully understand why God sent His son so that His children (us) could have a chance to get to heaven. Angels live with God, but they don't understand. Understanding is not a requirement. However, believing in Christ and directing our worship towards God is a requirement.

Saints
What Is a Saint?
The Bible makes several references to saints.
- Psalms 34:9 Fear the LORD, you his saints, for those who fear him lack nothing.
- Psalm 149: 1 Praise the LORD. Sing to the LORD a new song, his praise in the assembly of the saints.
- Psalm 149:4 For the LORD takes delight in his people; he crowns the humble with salvation.
- Psalm 149:5 Let the saints rejoice in this honor and sing for joy on their beds.

According to these passages, the implication is that a saint is someone who follows Christ. A believer is a person to be respected. However, worshipping a believer, even a good and powerful one, is still misdirected.

Some may frown on such a loose definition of saint. Some will feel that a religious governing body can only ordain a person to be a saint. No matter what definition is used, both definitions have been applied to the apostle Peter.

Peter

If we look at Peter for a moment, he was a strong soldier of Christ. (At least after the bird incident anyways; see Matthew 26). Peter was a good man, a powerful man, a man who had walked with Christ. He most likely commanded respect when entering a room. I am sure someone seeing him for the first time would be in awe and feel the need to worship him. However, no matter how good a person or saint Peter was, even Peter would not allow himself to be worshipped. His story relating to being worshipped can be seen in Acts 10:25, 26.

> Acts 10:25, 26 As Peter entered the house, Cornelius met him and fell at his feet in reverence. [26]But Peter made him get up. "**Stand up,**" he said, "**I am only a man myself.**"

Peter must have felt humbled by this interchange. Having another fall at his feet in reverence had to touch his heart. He could have let this act go to his head, but he did not. He told the man to get up because he too was only a man. If Peter had felt that being worshipped was OK, he would have let Cornelius lie there on the floor in front of him.

During one of my trips to Italy, I had the opportunity to visit Rome. What a place! During my visit, I was able to tour the Vatican. During the tour, we were directed to walk past a stature of Peter that was all in bronze. The statue is up on a pedestal and is of Peter sitting with his feet at about our shoulder height. We were told if we touch the foot of Peter, we would have good fortune. To my surprise, that foot was nearly warn off from the touches of 1000's of people looking for good fortune. I could not help but hear Peter saying, "I am only a man myself."

I am certainly no Peter, but several years ago my work took me to India. I made some phone calls and found that there were several there who were involved with the **Church that Christ Built**. Once I arrived in India, I looked up these people. My coworkers thought it was odd that I was meeting friends one night for dinner. They knew I had never been to India before, so how could I have friends there? The fact is that when you find members of **the Church that Christ Built**, you are never alone and you will always have a friend. Anyway, when we met, the missionaries told me they wanted me to preach on Sunday. They told me they did not want an American style 20-minute sermon. They wanted me to talk for at least an hour and preferably one-and-a-half hours. My mouth dropped open, but these guys were good. They told me that the Bible says we are to be ready in season and out of season to give an account. They were quoting scripture to me. So I agreed. I spent the next few nights preparing for my sermon. I ended up giving that sermon 3 times at 3 different churches. What an experience. However, in almost every church, when I would finish my lesson, I would find myself in the front of a line of small children. They wanted to meet me, touch my clothes, and for me to sign the few Bibles that they had. I was humbled, to say the least. I wanted so badly to tell them what Peter told Cornelius: I am nothing, you don't need my autograph, I am only a man. However, the missionaries told me I was being an encouragement to the kids. They told me that the kids don't get to see very many Christian Americans. So, I signed their Bibles with "Keep the Faith." I sure hope they have.

Moses and Elijah

Peter must have learned his lesson about whom to worship when God Himself reprimanded him. Can you imagine the unbelievable feeling Peter must have had to look up and see the Lord talking with Moses and Elijah? Peter would have spent much of his life learning and studying Moses and Elijah. Then to get to see them talking with the Lord. He must have felt like jumping out of his skin. I am sure Peter's intentions were noble when he suggested building an altar to recognize the Lord, Moses, and Elijah. However, God did not see it that way.

> Matthew 17:4-5 Peter said to Jesus, "Lord, it is good for us to be here. If you wish, I will put up three shelters – one for you, one for Moses and one for Elijah." [5]While he was still speaking, a bright cloud enveloped them, and a voice from the cloud said, "This is my Son, whom I love; with him I am well pleased. **Listen to him**!"

Modern Day Saints

All you have to do to find modern-day saints is to go to the Internet and type saint into the search engine. I was amazed at what I found. There were sites for saint of the day, most favorite saint, saint lookup tables, and on and on. I am all for learning about great men of the faith. However, we must be careful not to cross the line of worshipping them. I often see Saint "so and so" jewelry that people will wear. They will tell me that Saint "so and so" protects them or helps with this or that. I often think to myself, "Isn't Jesus supposed to look after us? Isn't God caring for us? Why do I need Saint so and so to help me out when I have Jesus?"

All of these questions came to mind when I was in Ireland a few years ago. Some of my Irish coworkers wanted me to stop by a church building. They said that since I was a "religious type," I should meet Saint Oliver Plunkett. I am still not sure how they knew I was religious. Since I had never met a saint, I decided to find this one.

When I finally found the building, I was quite shocked and surprised at what I saw. Off to the left and toward the front of this very old and large edifice was a brass structure with candles all around it. Sitting on the floor around this structure were several people deep in a form of prayer. As I got closer, I saw a glass box at eye level. Inside the box was the preserved head of Oliver Plunkett. I was quite taken back when I realized I was looking at an actual head in a glass box. I looked for some documentation and found that Oliver Plunkett had been a missionary in the 1600s. He must have been quite a speaker, because he made someone in a high place pretty mad. These officials cut off his head and burned his remains. When his church followers located where he had been burned, they found his head had not been consumed by fire. So they put it in a glass box and Mr. Plunkett has been preserved ever since.

Learning about great people of the faith is quite interesting and useful for understanding the struggles believers can go through. However, if we cross the line and worship them, we could disqualify ourselves from the prize. This is why I find the prayer that the literature had on it so disturbing.

"Prayer of St. Plunkett, Glorious Martyr, Oliver, who willingly gave your life for your faith, help us also to be strong in faith. May we be loyal like you to the Sea of Peter. By your intercession and example may all hatred and bitterness be banished from the hearts of Irish men and women. May the peace of Christ reign in our hearts, as it did in your heart, even at the moment of your death. Pray for us and for Ireland. Amen"

The prayer is asking Oliver to help their faith to be strong, to intercede for them when dealing with hatred and bitterness, and to pray for them as well as Ireland. Some may say this is not worship. However, as I saw people kneeling in front of this shrine, I could not help but see tears in the eyes of Christ. If this were not worship, then it was dangerously close. Christ died for our sins, not Mr. Plunkett. Christ wants us to talk to Him, not Mr. Plunkett; Christ will help us when we are down, not Mr. Plunkett; Christ intercedes for us, not Mr. Plunkett. Mr. Plunkett was a great man, but he is not worthy of taking the place of Christ or even standing in for Him. No one is . . .

Idols

What Is an Idol?
The dictionary defines an idol as follows:
- An image used as an object of worship.
- A false god, one that is adored, often blindly or excessively.
- Something visible but without substance.

Examining this definition, we see that an idol is a false god used as an object of worship that is often blindly adored yet has no substance.

Have you ever heard the term, "Give credit where credit is due?" Basically, if someone does something good, give them the credit for it. What typically happens, when person A does something nice to person B, and person B inturn gives the credit to person C, then person A can get pretty upset.

In that example, God is A, we are B, and idols are C. Our God is our creator. When a figure is worshiped, we are slapping God in the face and making Him mad. The following two passages give us insight into how God feels about false gods.

- Exodus 34: 14 Do not worship any other god, for the LORD, whose name is Jealous, is a jealous God.
- Deuteronomy 16:21 Do not set up any wooden Asherah pole beside the altar you build to the LORD your God, 22 and do not erect a sacred stone, for these the LORD your God hates.

The Bible is full of examples of people worshipping false gods. The Golden Calf described in Exodus 32:1-10 is a good example of how not to worship God.

Folly of Idol Worship
The Lord tells Isaiah that idols are powerless, they cannot save, they will mislead you, and they will profit a man nothing but shame. When God puts idol worship in this perspective, we need to make sure we don't fall into the trap of idol worship. In Isaiah 2:8, 17, 18, and 20-22, we see the folly of idol worship. In verse 17, we can gain insight into what God thinks about idol worship.

> Isaiah 2: 17 The **arrogance of man** will be brought low and the pride of men humbled;

Purge the Evil from Among You
A few years ago, I read a chronological Bible. A chronological Bible has all the stories put in order, based on time. This makes the Bible read more like a book. One of the phrases that struck me said to "purge the evil from among you." This phrase is a constant warning from God to His people. One example of this phrase is as follows:

> Deuteronomy 21: 18-21: A Rebellious Son
> [18] If a man has a stubborn and rebellious son who does not obey his father and mother and will not listen to them when they discipline him, [19] his father and mother shall take hold of him and bring him to the elders at the gate of his town. [20] They shall say to the elders, "This son of ours is stubborn and rebellious. He will not obey us. He is a profligate and a drunkard." [21] Then all the men of his town shall stone him to death. You must **purge the evil from among you**. All Israel will hear of it and be afraid.

This one was used on me a few times growing up, so maybe that is why it comes to mind. God does not tolerate evil. He does not want us to play with it or even be near it, especially when it comes to idols.

The Unknown God

On one of my trips to India, I had the opportunity to eat dinner at the home of one of my co-workers. During dinner, I noticed that on the top of each doorway there was a different figure. I did not think much of it until I noticed that each time my friend's wife went by one of them, she would give a slight bow. I had been a friend of this co-worker for quite some time, so I asked him what the figures were. He told me his wife was quite religious and felt the need to have a god overseeing each of the rooms of their apartment. I couldn't help thinking of the passage in Acts that refers to an unknown God.

> Acts 17:23 For as I walked around and looked carefully at your objects of worship, I even found an altar with this inscription: **TO AN UNKNOWN GOD**. Now what you worship as something unknown I am going to proclaim to you.

Paul noticed figures of gods as he walked through the town. The people were obviously religious and they did not want to leave any god out, so they added an alter to an unknown God. Paul used this figure to start his sermon on the one and only God.

While I was in India, I was able to talk with some Christians. They informed me that in America there is really very little competition for Christ. I asked what they meant. They told me that in India when they preach Christ to the locals, they are very receptive in a general way. They simply add Christ to the list of false gods they already have. To them, Christ is just another god. So the more of a collection of gods they can get, the more "holy" they appear. The missionary told me that getting them to believe only in Christ is quite a challenge.

As I pondered what I saw at my friend's house and what this missionary told me, I took my camera and started taking pictures of some of the images of false worship I could see while I was in India. I saw figures made of stone, wood, and bronze. The elephant idol happened to be very popular during my time in India. Someone claimed that this cement elephant had sipped milk from a jar they had placed near its nose. As a result of this claim, people had offered food to nearly every one of these elephant idols. The people I saw were so poor and had such little means, but they would rather give food to a cement image rather than take food for themselves. Then there were the cows. They were everywhere. They roam around like stray dogs. People leave food for them. In India, they believe in reincarnation. They feel that to come back as a cow is the highest honor. I asked one of my Indian co-workers why the cow was so special. He said it had something to do with the Golden Calf in the Bible.

I don't know if you have ever seen people give food, money, time, and prayer to a piece of wood, a piece of cement, or even an animal. But as I saw all of these images of worship, the passages in the Bible about God being a jealous God came to life. In my mind's eye, God was quite upset and I could once again see tears in the eyes of Christ.

Satan is a worthy advisory. He can convince entire nations to blindly adore false gods that have no substance. Please be careful.

Idols? Not Me!
Idols are the ultimate in Satan's bag of tricks. If he can get people to lose their focus on Christ and replace their zeal for hollow images, he will. In third world countries these images can be seen everywhere you go. However, what about in our back yard?

If idols are the ultimate in distractions, then distractions may be the first step toward idol worship. A few chapters ago, we did an exercise to track our time to find our "Christian" grade. If you had a chance to do that, what was your grade? I am afraid that mine was not that great. As I looked at my time in more detail, I found that the following areas were consuming my time: Work, exercise, eating out, sleeping, watching TV, playing with the kids, hobbies, home repair/remodeling, and attending worship. I was spending more time with my hobby of buying electric HO scale racing slot cars (if you have any, let me know) than I was studying about God. Actually, when I looked at the little bit of physical exercise I do, even that amount of time was more than the time I was spending with God. I hope you take a week and track your time. Time tracking can be a real eye opener. No matter what we say, our time gives us away. The phrase, "Where our treasure (time) is, there your heart will be also" really holds true.

Has Satan had the last laugh in America? We in America are too civilized for idol worship. We are too smart to fall for those tricks of old Satan. No way has Satan tricked us. Now pass me the remote - my favorite TV show is on. Satan is not partial to any one form of distraction to keep us from seeing God. If he can keep us out of the Bible and make us believe the life we are living or the church we are attending will get us into heaven, then he wins. He will try to use the tricks that work.

Worship Misguided
When I was in junior high, I ran cross-country. I use the term "ran" very loosely because distance running was not my strong suit. There was one runner who was not only our school's best runner, but also one of the top runners in our state. He was always first. My coach would tell the rest of us not to worry about the course; we should just follow our top runner. At the start of each

meet, our top runner would spend a lot of time talking with the track officials. I finally realized that if he got off track, the rest of us would follow him and we would all lose. Our intentions to do a good job in the race would be in place, but if the guy we were following went down the wrong path, we would all be disqualified.

Misguided worship is similar to this example. Misguided worship is typically the result of people trying to please God, yet doing so in a manner that is different than God wants. The following examples show how worship can be misguided by:
- Personal Preference
- Empty Worship
- Worship for Show

Personal Preference
Personal preference can be extremely hard to overcome. Even if we know we are wrong, change is difficult. The Bible warns of the problems with basing our belief on personal preference.

Appearance of Wisdom
The hardest personal preference to overcome is the one that actually seems right. I think this next story is valid. I read one time that the practice of bleeding a patient was commonly used in the 1700s. The doctors of the time thought that blood contained a bug that was making a person sick. So if the doctor could get rid of some of this blood, then the person should get better. This practice was applied to our first president, but he died from the procedure. We now see this as a flawed way of thinking. However, at the time, even respected physicians were following this practice. The Bible warns us of following philosophies that have no Biblical basis.
- Colossians 2:8 See to it that no one takes you captive through **hollow and deceptive philosophy**, which depends on **human tradition** and the **basic principles of this world** rather than on Christ.
- Colossians 2:20-23 [20]Since you died with Christ to the basic principles of this world, why, as though you still belonged to it, do you submit to its rules: [21]"Do not handle! Do not taste! Do not touch!"? [22]These are all destined to perish with use, because they are based on **human commands** and teachings. [23]Such regulations indeed have an **appearance of wisdom**, with their **self-imposed worship**, their **false humility** and their **harsh treatment** of the body, but they lack any value in restraining sensual indulgence.

The term "basic principles of this world" means false, worldly, religious, and elementary teachings. Paul was counteracting the Colossian heresy, which in part, taught that for salvation one needed to combine faith in Christ with secret knowledge and with man-made regulations concerning such physical and external practices as circumcision, eating and drinking, and observance of religious festivals.

A friend of mine that had been on military duty in Iraq was telling me about a parade he saw firsthand. In this parade, the men were hitting themselves in the head with swords as they walked by the onlookers. They were making themselves bloody to show their allegiance and dedication to their god. Hitting one's self in the head with a sword to demonstrate religious conviction is the definition of "harsh treatment". This is the very same act that Paul warned us to stay away from nearly 2,000 years ago.

Paul Opposes Peter
Even Peter had a personal preference that was standing in the way of his ministry. Paul had to work with Peter to resolve this problem.

> Galatians 2:11-14 [11]When Peter came to Antioch, I opposed him to his face, because he was **clearly in the wrong**. [12]Before certain men came from James, he used to eat with the Gentiles. But when they arrived, he began to draw back and separate himself from the Gentiles because he was afraid of those who belonged to the circumcision group. [13]The other Jews joined him in his hypocrisy, so that by their hypocrisy even Barnabas was led astray. [14]When I saw that they were **not acting in line with the truth** of the gospel, I said to Peter in front of them all, "You are a Jew, yet you live like a Gentile and not like a Jew. How is it then, that you force Gentiles to follow Jewish customs?"

Peter got the point and resolved the problem. However, his change was the result of harsh words that were necessary to break a personal preference.

Ghost Month
Several years ago, I went to Singapore for a business trip. While I was there, I noticed several people in the parking lot of our company burning items in a large crate. I at first thought there was a riot taking place. However, none of my coworkers seemed to notice anything out of the ordinary. I asked why there were people burning items in the parking lot. They said, "Oh, this is today's Ghost month activity." Thinking this was enough of an answer, they left it at that. However, they only sparked my curiosity. So I asked, "What is Ghost month?" I was looked at like I was from another planet. I told the guys that back home we don't have a Ghost month. Finally, they told me more of this festival. This is how the story went.

Ghost month is designed to take care of those who have died someplace other than their home. The thought is that these people who have died outside their home spend eternity lost and trying to find their home. So in order to keep these lost souls from causing problems, those that are still alive are to give these lost souls food, clothes, and money to help in their search. The way the lost souls get these gifts is by burning them. So in the large crate you saw different types of food, clothes, and money. I happened to notice that the money was actually play money. When I saw the play money, I spoke before I thought. I remarked, "I did not know they used play money in the afterlife." Note to any world travelers - never ever make fun of a local custom.

One of the students took me aside and informed me this was no joke. In fact, his grandmother who had died several years ago was fortunate to have his mother. He told me that as his grandmother was about to die in the hospital, the mother insisted that they fill the grandmother with air. They then rushed the grandmother to their home and allowed her to exhale. The grandmother was officially pronounced dead at her home. This guy was as serious as he could be. He was thankful that his mother had saved his grandmother from the plight of those lost souls.

Once again, in my mind's eye I could see tears in the eyes of Christ. After hearing the Ghost month story, I became aware of activities all over town. Nearly everywhere I went there were food trays with flares burning in them sitting on the curb. I could not help but think of the passage in Galatians related to special days.

Galatians 4:10-11 You are observing special days and months and seasons and years! [11]**I fear for you**.

I Like It This Way
I was driving to work with a co-worker one day when the subject of religion came up. For some reason the guy driving told me he did not like going to a particular church because of the frequency with which they performed a certain act of worship. He told me that he much preferred his church's method because they do that act only once a year. In his mind, that made the act more sacred.

I'll talk later about what the act was, but for now let's look at this person's mental database. In his mind, what was his justification for his actions? Basically, he liked the way his church performed the act. He had no Biblical evidence to support his conclusion other than, "I like it this way." When I tried to talk with him about his view and even share with him scriptures that clearly contradict his view, he would not listen. In fact, the conversation changed very quickly.

No matter what our personal preference, if our preference is not aligned with the Scriptures then we are in danger of being wrong. If the Creator of the universe tells us what He wants, shouldn't we find a way to give Him exactly what he asks?

Empty Worship

The idea of going through the motions of worship because we have to and not because we want to is referred to as empty worship. Matthew warns of this behavior in the following Biblical passage:

> Matthew 15:7-9 [7]**You hypocrites!** Isaiah was right when he prophesied about you: [8]These people honor me with their lips, but their hearts are far from me. [9]They **worship me in vain**; their teachings are but **rules taught by men**."

God finds it quite odd that we humans often listen to "rules taught by men", rather than to the original designer, Himself! Worship based on human traditions is vain worship. What do you think of when you hear the word vain? A few thoughts that come to mind are of an empty, shallow, inward focus. I seem to recall a Carly Simon song, "You're So Vain." When you tie this word to worship, you get the image of someone who is just going through the motions. Their hearts and minds are disengaged.

For more than 15 years, I drove nearly an hour to and from work every day. I am almost afraid to admit this, but on more than one occasion I would get within a few miles of my house and realize I had no recollection of the trip. My brain had gone into autopilot. Maybe this type of "autopilot" is what God calls empty or vain worship. How often do we sing a hymn and then not remember the words, get upset if the service does not end on time, doze off during a long prayer, or not recall the preacher's sermon on the way out of the church parking lot? I am afraid I can say this has happened to me more than once. Sure, I can give you a list of reasons for my lack of attention. However, no matter what the reason, I fell into the trap of honoring God with my lips, while my heart was turned off.

God wants us to be engaged while we worship Him. The world, and consequently our worship service, can be full of distractions, but we need to fight them off and focus on what is going on while we worship God. God deserves our attention. When we allow distractions to block God's words from our hearts, we have given Satan a foothold. Vain, empty worship does nothing to strengthen our "Christian batteries." Just showing up for service, sitting there, and leaving without allowing God's word to enter our hearts does nothing to strengthen our faith. As a result, we can leave the worship service vulnerable to the darts of Satan. This vulnerability is why God frowns on empty worship. He wants us to be as spiritually strong as possible.

Worship for Show

"Watch me, Watch me." That is what we heard for several weeks as our daughter was taking our new dog to puppy school. One of the commands was "Watch me." When my daughter would say that command, the dog was supposed to stop what it was doing and look her in the eye. I did not think our dog would ever get it. However, my daughter did not give up. Now, it is a little weird. When she says, "Watch me," the little dog stops in his tracks and follows her eyes wherever she goes.

Another phrase I get to hear quite often is, "Dad, did you see that?" I would hear this from my son when he was learning to skateboard. Once he learned a new trick he would quickly turn to see if I saw him do it. Recognition for success is not necessarily a problem. Inside, and sometimes outside, we are screaming with phrases like "Watch me" and "Did you see that?" The problem comes when these phrases show up in worship.

Theatrics

The Bible warns of worship practices that are performed by individuals for the purpose of being seen. The expression "to be seen" translates from the Greek term *theathenai,* which is the basis of our modern word "theater."

> Matthew 6: 1-2 [1]"Be careful not to do your "acts of righteousness" before men, **to be seen** by them. If you do, you will have **no reward** from your Father in heaven.
> [2]"So when you give to the needy, do not announce it with trumpets, as the hypocrites do in the synagogues and on the streets, to be **honored by men**. I tell you the truth, they have received their reward in full.

When you think of the word theater, what comes to mind? I think of actors, acting, fancy costumes, orchestrated stage positioning, orchestras, and the like. The theater is a magical place that allows one to escape reality and be entertained for a short period of time.

This is a problem when worship is done with a theatrical theme. Entertainment becomes the measure of a quality service rather than the communion with our Lord. In the scripture above, Matthew warns of people who do their Christian acts in order to be seen and honored by men. Those who get caught in this trap run the risk of losing their reward with their Father in heaven. We have to be careful that our worship is not for men, but for God. Anyone who gets in front of a group of people in a worship setting has to be careful not to be using the "Watch me" phrase we just talked about. The people in front of the congregation have to be as transparent as possible in order to let the *message* stir the people, not the *theatrics* of the person. The Word of God is powerful; theatrics are not needed to make the Word stronger.

Talent

When I was in Singapore, the church I was attending found out I could lead songs. They asked me to lead a few songs the following Sunday. I was quite nervous about it; I did not want to become the focus of the worship. I wanted the message of the songs to touch their hearts. After the service, a lady came up to me and thanked me for the songs. I did not quite know what to say. She continued with, "I could see the love of Jesus in your song leading." That probably was the best compliment anyone has ever given me. By being transparent in a public manner, the word of God was preached more clearly through the songs we were singing.

Have you ever heard someone say something like the following?

"I have a God given talent to _____(fill in the blank). If I can't use it in worship, then I do not feel I have done an adequate job of serving God."

I always get an uneasy feeling when I hear this phrase. It sounds a little like my son when he asks, "Did you see that?" Do people who use this comment want to be a conduit for God's word or an actor in front of a crowd? I am sure that not all people who say this fall into the "to be seen" category, but apparently there were several people who fell into that trap in the first century. Otherwise, Matthew would not be telling them to stop.

What theatrics did Christ use when he preached? Yes, he did miracles, but often He would ask that the recipients of the miracle keep the gift to themselves. When we are proclaiming the Word of God in a public manner of worship, we have to be careful not to add so much pizzazz that we distract from the message.

Power Point is a software program for making presentations. When I first started using it, my presentations were full of animation, fancy slide transitions, words popping in and out, sound clips, and so on. After one presentation, a customer came up to me and asked me a ton of questions related to how I was able to get power point to do all those neat tricks. We talked for several minutes on how to use this software. However, once we were done I realized he never asked about the content of the presentation, just the show. Hence, the problem with pizzazz. We can get so caught up with fancy that we miss the message.

Finding better ways to present the message of Christ is not wrong. When I started teaching I used white chalk and a chalkboard. When we got colored chalk, we were quite excited. Then we went from chalk to whiteboards with erasable color markers. Eventually we progressed to electronic media with tools like Power Point. Each technological improvement allowed us to convey material faster and better. However, we must be careful we don't cross the line into pizzazz. What good is the content if the audience can't see through all the fluff? I know that finding the line between preaching God's word and entertaining with God's word can be difficult. That does not mean we should not try. If we have crossed the line into entertaining, Matthew tells us we will lose the prize.

Structures
On one particular business trip, I went to Sweden. This trip was in the winter and was near a huge mountain ski resort. My contact wanted to take me to the mountains when I arrived. We had a nice lunch at one of the small towns on the mountain. Then, he wanted to take me up to see a cathedral. We walked for some distance with snow skiers everywhere around us. Then in the distance, I saw this colossal structure. I could tell my guide was quite excited. As we got closer, there was a flurry of people going in and out of the building. Walking through the front door, we entered a huge open building with church pews in the center and a walking track around them. On the walls were the most elaborate paintings I had ever seen. Very famous painters had done them all. The supporting structures in the building were covered with gold. The room was a bit chilly with an eerie silence. In fact, there were people walking around making sure that there was no photography and no talking. Once we made it around the building, we were escorted outside. On the outside of the building, there were souvenir shops so you could purchase trinkets and mementos of this impressive building.

My guide was quite proud for taking me to this cathedral. He asked me what I thought. I was a little slow on my response. My guide said, "I thought you were a religious person? Did you not feel the presence of God in that building?" I looked at him and said, "I am a religious person, but that building made me sad." He was very puzzled and asked me to explain. Here is what I said. "The decorations, the fancy interior, the paintings, the temperature, the silence, and the vastness of the open space are all architectural wonders. These wonders are designed to create a feeling of awe. The hope is that we will get a feeling for the might of God and our insignificance. Being in awe of our God is a good thing. The problem with getting that feeling from a building is that the feeling is not grounded in anything. God does not need a building to artificially make us feel how great He is." I then asked my guide to look at those mountains over there. "God's power and might are more evident in those mountains than this building. Also, this building must have cost millions of dollars to make and is full of priceless art work, but the location of the building is up on a mountain that we can get to only by foot. This does not seem like a good use of money." In fact, the day of my visit was a Sunday, yet the number of actual worshipers was quite small, even though there were thousands of people skiing all around.

I doubt that my guide expected to get a sermon. However, he did remark he had never heard anyone say things like I was saying. I thanked him for taking me to that place. However, I was sad when I was in that building. I am afraid I did not experience the awe and wonder of God. What I experienced was a deep feeling of sadness and once again I could see tears in the eyes of Christ.

God never said to build a *building* to go into all the world and preach the gospel - He told *us* to go into all the world and preach the gospel. I can't help but contrast that million-dollar facility with the hut I got to preach in while in India. In the million-dollar facility, a clever architect generated the presence of God. When I taught a Bible class to a packed house in a mud hut in India, followers of Christ generated the presence of God.

Artificial Feelings
The problem with showy worship is two-fold. One problem is making people the worship focus rather than God. The other is the artificial feeling generated by the show concerning God's might and power.

When I was in grade school, I read a mystery book. In that book, everyone was sure that a particular building was haunted. The sleuth started looking for clues as to why this building was so scary. He found that the building had been an old theater with a pipe organ. The owner of the building liked to play jokes on nosey kids who went into his building. He would play low frequency notes that were lower than the human ear can detect. These tones were so low that they actually caused the human body to resonate. The brain deciphered this sensation as fear. The nosey kids would take off.

I suppose the same sense of fear comes when watching a scary show. The music is designed to create a sense of fear. If you take that out of the picture, the show often becomes less scary. The sensation of fear is very real. However, the source of the fear is artificial. God hardly needs artificial stimulus in order for the power of His Word to be felt. He needs followers to read His Book.

Several years ago, I visited a friend's church. During the prayers, I could hear a choir start singing. They started off very faint, but grew louder or softer depending on the content of the prayer. When the prayer was nearly finished, the choir went into full force and the congregation went wild. I am afraid I did not go wild. I was reminded of artificial stimulus used to invoke emotion. I asked myself a few questions: Why did that choir need to add emphasis to the guy giving the prayer? Did God need sound to make the prayer more effective? How did the choir know when to get soft, when to get loud, and when to hit the high points? Why did the congregation get so wild when the prayer was finished? If you go to a church that practices worship in this way, then your mental database may be programmed to see this as normal. The line between entertainment and worship is not always easy to define. However, as I was thinking over these questions, it dawned on me that this prayer had been choreographed. Some will argue that, choreographed or not, the result of the combined choir and prayer got people to feel in touch with their Savior. Maybe, but choreographed worship sounds a lot like theater. We must be careful. Showy worship leads down a dangerous path. Just look at the example of the Pharisee and the tax collector in Luke.

> Luke 18:9-14 [9]To some who were confident of their own righteousness and looked down on everybody else, Jesus told this parable: [10]"Two men went up to the temple to pray, one a Pharisee and the other a tax collector. [11]The Pharisee stood up and prayed about himself: 'God, I thank you that I am not like other men—robbers, evildoers, adulterers—or even like this tax collector. [12]I fast twice a week and give a tenth of all I get.'
> [13]"But the tax collector stood at a distance. He would not even look up to heaven, but beat his breast and said, **'God, have mercy on me, a sinner.'**
> [14]"I tell you that this man, rather than the other, went home justified before God. For everyone who exalts himself will be humbled, and he who humbles himself will be exalted."

The **Church that Christ Built** does not need theatrics or clever programs to artificially create strong emotions related to the power of God. God is powerful enough with only His written Word. Worship for show is to be avoided. However, this is not to imply that church worship is to be boring. On the contrary, once distractions are removed from our worship, we can more clearly see the power and might of God. The intensity and gravity His Word can have on our heart are powerful, strong, and wonderful that boring is hardly the right description.

Closing Comments

As we come to a close in this chapter, we find that God wants us to stay away from two primary worship woes: Worship Misdirected or Worship Misguided.

Misdirected worship is a form of worship that attempts to direct our attention to something other than the true and living God. God is a jealous God. He can't stand to see us ask for help from anyone or anything but Him. He knows that only He can truly be of help to us when we are in trouble. God is not afraid of fake gods. He knows they are nothing. However, He loves us and wants us to follow His commands. When He sees us going after fake gods, our Father in heaven hurts. We are usually quick to point out that we don't follow fake gods. However, we have to be on our guard. Satan is quite the trickster. Just the other day I was reading a funny and in the last frame, the cartoon said, "if you listen real close, you can hear the gods laugh." I thought to myself, sorry about that, God. Satan is the master at working misdirection into our everyday lives.

Misguided worship is a form of worship to God that does not truly engage the hearts of the worshipers. God does not like or even hear this type of worship. The main problem with misguided worship is that it does not build a solid foundation for depending on Christ. Anyone can fall into the trap of misguided worship. The problem is that when difficult times come, we don't have a deep sense and appreciation for the power of almighty God. God does not want a faith that is strong only when we are in a building. He wants a faith that will stand when we are the only one. Misguided worship attacks the core of being a Christian: our faith.

God is looking for true worshipers. Those who seek His will do worship Him in spirit and truth. Are we His true worshipers actively seeking His will? Carving away worship styles that God clearly does not like helps us to more clearly see worship styles that He requires.

Questions to Consider
1. Read Isaiah 44:6-23 and right down 5 things about Idol worship that upset God.
2. If someone walked by your worship service, would they think they were witnessing a funeral or a party?
3. What feeling would strangers take with them after worship service?
4. How much of the annual budget of your church goes toward modernization of the worship experience?
5. Do you have an angel lapel pin? If so, why?
6. What distractions cause us to lose focus in the worship service? What can we do to avoid the trap of empty worship?
7. Is it wrong to have nice things? Can nice things become idols?

Chapter 5: Mind of Worship

Here Is Your Order?

I am not sure if it is just me, my family, or if this is a common problem. However, when I drive up to a drive-thru window and the person gives me a bag of food and says, "Here is your order," I really think this should be said in the form of a question. Either there is a tomato on my daughter's hamburger, lettuce on my son's taco, or worse yet, a missing order of French fries. These little errors may seem like small ones, but they usually start a flurry of discussions on what we should do next. Often I am already heading down the road. So turning around is not a good option. We should have just waited and checked the order before leaving, but I hate to do that, especially when there is a line of angry people trying to get their French fries. This little scenario happens more than I would like to count. The end result usually is that I did not get my order, and my family is not happy. I wonder how often God feels the same way when we mess up His order. He gave us specific instructions concerning the **Church that Christ Built**. Shouldn't we try to get them right? In this chapter, we will study the attitude we should have while we are worshiping our God.

Spirit Directed

In the last chapter, we found the word for worship most commonly translated from Greek was proskuneo, which means to "kiss toward." When we are worshiping, we are literally to kiss toward God. In Psalms 2:12, we actually see a similar phrase, Kiss the Son, literally used:

Three-Fold Worship

So what makes God happy? How do we kiss toward God? In order to answer those questions, let's find out whom the Father seeks in John 4:23. Why would you look for something that you did not need? Have you ever misplaced your wallet? I have and that is not a pleasant feeling. All my credit cards, ID, and money are in my wallet. If I misplace it, I literally turn the house upside down to find it. In other words, I really seek out my wallet. The same passion that I have in finding my wallet would almost come close to matching how God seeks true worshipers. If we look at this passage a little closer, we see that there are three elements to worship.

1. There is an object of worship and that is God.
2. There is an appropriate attitude of worship and that is with spirit.
3. There is a correct action to worship and that is truth.

God must have liked these three elements, because we see almost an exact copy of them in Joshua 24:14 "Now, therefore, fear Jehovah and serve him in sincerity and in truth." So what is a "true worshiper?" These passages indicate that a true worshiper is one who fears the Lord, is sincerely trying to please

Him, has a spirit that is excited to be in God's presence, and strives to truthfully follow His words. Wrapping all these together gives us new meaning to the term "kiss toward" God.

If we dig a little further into the Bible, we will find several passages that help us understand what it means to "kiss toward" God. Each will be discussed in detail:

- Submission/Reverence: 2 Kings 17:36; Revelation 14:7
- Humbled by God's Greatness: Psalms 66:1-4
- Gratitude: Psalms 95:1-6; Psalms 100:2, Revelation 5:9-14
- Utter Dependence: Psalms 95:6
- Only the Best for our God: Deuteronomy 26:10
- Obedience to God: Genesis 22:5
- Living Sacrifice: Romans 12:1

Submission/Reverence

Submission is one of the words that men like to use and women hate to hear. However, I think men may not be using the term correctly. In Ephesians 5: 21-33 the word submit used 4 times in three different applications.

- We are to submit to one another.
- Wives are to submit to their husbands.
- Church is to submit to Christ.

Milk Bucket vs. Fine China

Does submit mean that we are to do whatever anyone asks of us? Is our wife to be our "go for"? ("Honey, go for this, or Honey, go for that.") Look at how Christ talks about His church. He gave Himself up for the church, yet this passage says the church is to submit to Christ. This almost sounds backwards. These passages do seem backwards if we think of submission as a one-way street. I once heard a good definition of submission. Imagine that you have a piece of very expensive china and an old milk bucket. Both of these vessels can hold liquid, but which one would you handle with a little more care? If you drop the old milk bucket, you have not lost much. However, if you mishandle the fine china you could break an irreplaceable piece. That is not to imply that the fine china is fragile; on the contrary, the fine china is priceless.

What if we replace the term submission with the way we would treat a piece of fine china? Would this make a difference in how we read Ephesians chapter 5?

- Treat one another as though everyone is priceless.
- Husbands, treat your wife as though she is priceless.
- Christ, treat the church as though it is priceless.

How would you treat your neighbors knowing both are priceless? Husbands, how would you treat your wife knowing she is not replaceable? Christians, how does it make you feel knowing that Christ will take care of us? A few possible feelings, emotions, or actions that come to my mind are respect, appreciation, kind gestures, protection, and pride.

What wouldn't you do for a friend who treated you like this? Wives, what wouldn't you do for a husband who treated you like a queen? Christians, what should we do for a Christ who died for us? When submission is viewed in this way, hopefully the definition becomes clear. Submission does not mean to power over someone. Submission means to have a responsibility to treat others with respect, to make our wife feel honored to belong to her husband, to make Christians strive to search out the ways of our Lord.

Submit to the Lord

In the Old Testament, we see that Israelites were told they must submit to the Lord in 2 Kings 17:35-39. When we realize or appreciate what Christ did for us, submitting to His will is not a problem, but an obligation. Christ does not want a false submission. He does not want followers who go through the motions of faith or worship. He wants worshipers who strive to submit to His teachings from the depth of their being. Why? Because of a love that transcends understanding, Christ died for us. After all, salvation is priceless.

Humbled by God's Greatness

Brush with Fame

Have you ever had a brush with fame? A few years ago my wife and I were at Disney World when our brush with fame happened. We were walking down one of the streets when I saw this man who looked familiar. I told my wife and we started to get excited. So, we backed up and tried to pass this person again. After our second pass, we were pretty sure this person was famous. So, we backed up and passed again. Yep, that makes three passes. This time my wife asked one of the people with this person if he was Michael Landon? At that point, Mr. Landon turned to us and said, "Yes, but I am with my family." He was kind, but basically he told us to bug off. Kim and I felt quite embarrassed for bothering him. He was with his family at Disney World and we should have left him alone. The problem is, we had grown up watching his TV shows and were anxious to meet him, almost like a magnet pulling us toward a train wreck.

Maybe you have had a similar experience. I can remember another example when I was a kid on vacation with my parents. I was looking at some souvenirs when I noticed my parents trying to get my attention. I thought their action was strange and that something must be wrong. I went over to them and they asked, "Did you see the person you were standing next to?" I told them I had no idea who it was. Apparently, I was standing next to a famous lady who had been on a TV show they had seen. Since I had not seen the show, her presence next to me meant nothing.

Maybe these two examples aren't the greatest in the world, but in the first example, Kim and I were in awe of a TV and movie star. In the second example, the lady was just as famous, but I had no idea who she was. So her presence did not cause me to act silly. I don't think it is too much of a stretch, but these examples are a little like the relationship many of us have with God. Those who know God are in awe of his power and might, and we strive to follow him. However, those who have never met Him don't realize who He is and are unaffected by His presence.

All Earth Bow Down

The Bible gives us an idea of how we are supposed to act when we realize we are in the presence of God in Psalms 66:1-4. Look at the words in this passage: Shout, glory, praise, awesome, great, cringe, bow, and sing. These are all actions that "all the earth" is to do in the presence of God. "Wow" comes to mind. The earth is a big place, yet even "all the earth" is to get excited about God. Can you begin to imagine the power and might of God that He is able to command the respect of "all the earth"? When we begin to realize that God is for real, we cannot help but be quickly humbled by His greatness.

Be Happy

The Rookie

In the movie "The Rookie," Dennis Quaid plays a real life baseball player, Jim Morris, who made it to the big leagues later in life. Jim had been a high school teacher and baseball coach. He had a mean fastball when he was in college, but for some reason he did not try out for professional baseball. He would regularly pitch batting practice to his team and his guys felt he should try out for the pros. He refused, thinking he was too old at nearly 35. However, his team would not give up. They made a deal with him that if they could win so many games that year, then he would have to try out. He agreed and, as it turns out, they won that season. So he had to try out. The scouts could not believe the speed of his fastball. They could not comprehend someone at Jim's age throwing a ball that hard. They eventually gave him the OK and signed him on to a minor league team. He played on that team and eventually made it to the big leagues where he played for 2 years. The Internet has a nice write up on this story, starting with this comment from Jim: "I consider myself very lucky. God has a funny way of bringing some things around and knocking you in the head with the ultimate destination. Something I should have achieved quite easily took me a long time to get around to. It came in His time, not mine."

In my opinion, this is a great movie and quite the tearjerker. Mr. Morris and I are close to the same age, I was rooting for him all the way. I have said all this to lead up to one comment in the movie that stood out. Jim was playing in the minor leagues and the accommodations were not that great. Most of his teammates were grumbling and complaining about the situation. However, Jim was quite content and even happy. As he got ready to go out onto the field, he went to the guys that were complaining and with a grin on his face said, "We get to play baseball today!"

Why was Jim not joining in with the complaining? Most likely he knew he was given a chance of a lifetime to play the game he loved. The surroundings did not sidetrack him; he was getting to play baseball. Just because everyone else was complaining, that was not a reason for him to complain. He got to play ball. What a great attitude and a great lesson for us.

We Get to Go to Church!

All too often, we get sidetracked with worship. Maybe the preacher's lesson was a little off, or the song leader messed up, or the carpet is dirty, or the little kid in front of us made too much noise, or you stayed up too late and can't stay awake. Whatever it is, we sometimes forget that we get to go to worship. Did you catch that, "We get to go to worship!" In some countries, worshiping God is against the law, but for many of us we actually get to worship Him. How awesome a concept - we get the privilege of worshiping the almighty God!

Just as Jim refused to complain with his teammates, we should refuse to complain concerning worship. Jim saw past the shortcomings of the minor leagues and could see the awesome gift he was given to be able to play baseball. We must have the same attitude toward worshiping God. We cannot lose focus of the awesome gift we have been given. We get to worship God! The feeling of joy related to worshiping God is what Psalms 100:2 is talking about.

Worship the Lord with **gladness**; come before him with joyful songs.

Utter Dependence

Wild Ride

During the BK time in my married life, my wife and I decided to go whitewater rafting. (By the way, BK stands for "Before Kids.") Maybe we were young and dumb - I am not sure - but we thought we would have a good time. In preparation for the event, the whitewater company divided all the people into groups and assigned each group a guide. The guide is trained to navigate the river and provide a safe trip through the rapids. Prior to hitting any rapids, he also taught us how to paddle as a team and how to react in difficult situations. Our team listened intently to our guide and we grew to depend on him completely. We actually had gotten pretty good, so good that the other teams would let ours be the first to find the safest route through a particularly difficult rapid. The foam from the river would be flying everywhere, the rapids swirling around us and going in and over the boat. The roar was amazing, but we would focus on our guide, trusting his every word. Nearly every time, we made difficult rapids look easy. When we came out the other side victorious, we would wait for the other teams to hit the rapids. Almost always some team would capsize and there would be people and paddles everywhere. We would help retrieve them. Maybe we got overconfident, maybe we got careless, or maybe the guide wanted to show off a little. Nevertheless, bad things were around the next bend. Just ahead there were two clear passages down the river. One was nice, calm, and about 40 feet wide. The other was a strong whitewater rapid about 2 feet wide. The obvious choice was the 40-foot wide side of the river. However, the 2-foot wide choice seemed a better one to our guide. He told us to head for the gap. That should have been our first clue. A 5-foot wide raft and a 2-foot wide gap with large rocks on both sides don't mix. However, we were the "A-team," we were invincible, we trusted our guide, and our guide said "Go for the 2-foot gap." So we did. As we got to the point of no return, the guide told us that on his command we would have to all get on one side of the raft so that we could slide through this small opening. At this point, the blood starts to really move. We were so focused, and we were going so fast. Then we heard the command, "left side now." We responded like robots. We all hit the left side; the raft went up like one of those trick cars on two side wheels. We were good. Then our luck ran out. The guide forgot one small command. He forgot to tell us to get back in our places once through the gap. When we came out the other side, the raft flipped over in the middle of a roaring white water rapid, in the midst of huge rocks. We were all thrown from the raft and I was immediately sucked under. All that I could see was feet and bubbles everywhere. I was rolling and tumbling and had no idea which way was up. Luckily, I was wearing a life jacket. I held on and hoped I would go toward the surface. Eventually I got there. Almost all of us were everywhere, our stuff was floating down the river, and the other rafts were picking up our belongings. There was one problem: As I scanned the surface, I could not find my wife. Now I started to panic. As it turns out, she came up under the raft. That is a bad place to be when you think you are drowning. Fortunately, her dad was in our group and they both came up at about the same time. He knew what was happening and was able to calm Kim down and help her get out from under this raft. When I finally saw them, I was very relieved. Once we all got back in the raft, we were quite shaken, feeling a strong sense of betrayal. We had put our faith in our guide and he had let us down.

We had unfounded faith in our guide that we would make that small opening. The thought of failure never entered our mind. I can't believe how quickly we came to depend so deeply on a complete stranger. God is our guide, he will not lead us into waters we cannot handle. In Psalms 95:6, we find that we are under His care.

Worry Gauge

God will never lead us down a path that we cannot pass. We have a God who knows what we need before we do. Matthew 6:25-34 is one of my favorite passages about a subject that I do way too often. In this passage, we are shown how silly it is for us to worry. We are so much more important to God than birds and flowers, but God takes care of them. Why would we ever think that He would not take care of us? We also see that the "you" in this passage refers to those who seek Him first. Could it be that the amount of worry in our life is directly related to the relationship we have with God? If our support system is based on people or ourselves, then we will fall short and have good reason to worry. However, when our support system is based on God, then we have a guide who will not let us down, will take care of us, and who is worthy of our utter dependence. What is the source of our confidence, God or flesh?

> Philippians 3:3 . . . we who worship by the Spirit of God, who glory in Christ Jesus, and who **put no confidence in the flesh**.

Obedience to God, Without Question!

What does it mean to depend so completely on God? Utter dependence means that we will obey Him without question. We have such a strong personal relationship with God that no matter what happens in our life, we know that He will provide. I have heard it said that if you pray for rain, you should carry an umbrella.

Abraham

One of the greatest examples of utter dependence can be found in the story of Abraham and Isaac. This is one of those Biblical stories that I have a hard time understanding. Isaac had been given to Abraham and Sarah late in life. God had promised Abraham that his descendents would be more numerous than the sands on the seashore. However, God asked Abraham to offer Isaac as a sacrifice in Genesis 22:2. Abraham would have had every reason to argue with God. However, he did not. Some have said that Abraham's relationship with God was so strong that he figured God would raise Isaac from the dead. We can catch a glimpse of Abraham's faith when he tells his servant in Genesis 22:5 that he and the boy will go up to offer a sacrifice and that they would both come back. What must have been going through Abraham's mind? I cannot imagine. Then his son asks him, "Where is our sacrifice?" Isaac was no stranger to sacrifices. He would have known that they did not have anything to offer. Abraham tells him that God will provide. However, in verses 9-10, Isaac must have gotten the picture when his dad put him on the altar and took out his knife.

If I were Abraham, I would have been thinking, "OK God, when can we call this off?" However, we get no indication that Abraham ever wavered. He took out his knife with the intention of ending his son's life. As he started to plunge the knife in the direction of his son, verses 11-12 show us that an Angel told him to stop. Abraham must have been relieved beyond imagination. He must have had tears running down his face as he took his son off the altar. Utter obedience . . . What has God asked of us?

King Saul

King Saul could have been great. However, he failed when it came to complete obedience to God. The story of his demise starts in 1 Samuel 15 and has to do with Saul not completely destroying a group of people known as the Amalekites. In order to fully appreciate why Saul was so severely punished by God for his act of disobedience, we need to understand why God wanted the Amelekites destroyed in the first place. In Exodus 17: 8-14, we see that these people picked a fight with God's chosen nation. This was a bad move on their part.

> Exodus 17: 14
> [14] Then the LORD said to Moses, "Write this on a scroll as something to be remembered and make sure that Joshua hears it, because **I will completely blot out the memory of Amalek from under heaven.**"

As a kid reading this fight story in Bible school, I always found it interesting. Moses actually had to hold his hands up in order to win the fight. I always wondered if Moses had a sense of humor and flapped his arms like a chicken. Probably not, but we see that once Moses got some help holding up his arms, the Israelites won the fight. This fight must have been important to the Lord. He made sure that Moses recorded His revenge so that it would be remembered. He was going to blot out the memory of the Amalekites. That is a strong threat, but the Lord never backs down on a threat. The Amalekites were doomed, but in God's time. Nearly 400 years after the threat had been made, it was time to fulfill the promise. The person told to carry out the demise of the Amalekites was King Saul.

> 1 Samuel 15: 2-3 [2] This is what the LORD Almighty says: 'I will punish the Amalekites for what they did to Israel when they waylaid them as they came up from Egypt. [3] Now go, attack the Amalekites and **totally destroy everything that belongs to them. Do not spare them; put to death men and women, children and infants, cattle and sheep, camels and donkeys.**' "

God is still upset with them and He wants them removed from the face of the earth. Can you imagine? God wants nothing left to remind Him of these bullies that picked on His children. Who do you want on your side? This message to

Saul was very clear. We see in 1 Samuel 15:7-9 that Saul got the message and set out to fulfill the command, but he did not follow the instructions. He spared everything that was good. Come on, Saul, what were you thinking? Surely he had not forgotten God's command already, yet he did not follow it. In fact, verse 9 says he was unwilling to comply. This was a really bad decision on Saul's part. God was not happy.

> 1 Samuel 15:10 [10] Then the word of the LORD came to Samuel: [11] "I am **grieved** that I have made Saul king, because **he has turned away from me** and **has not carried out my instructions.**" Samuel was troubled, and he cried out to the LORD all that night.

God must have been eager to see his command fulfilled. He had waited a long time to realize His revenge on these bullies. Then, Saul goes and messes up. God tells Samuel He is grieving over his decision to make Saul king. Can you imagine God being upset? Well, He was in this case. God was grieved because Saul had turned away from Him and had not carried out His instructions. How sad. Do you suppose God grieves for us when we don't follow His instructions? In 1 Samuel 15:12-17 we see that after Samuel got the message from God, he set out to find Saul. When he found him, he asked the question we should try never to be asked, "Why did you not obey the LORD?"

Look what Saul was doing. He made a monument in his image. This sure sounds like he was getting a big head. Samuel finally caught Saul, and look what Saul said when they met, "I have carried out the Lord's instructions." Wait a minute. God said wipe out everything, but Saul has the King and the best of all the animals. Yet he was telling Samuel he had "carried out the Lord's instructions." Was he lying or did he talk himself into believing that what he did was right? In either case, he was wrong. We must be careful not to fall into the same trap. If we don't like what God tells us to do, we don't have the right to think our lack of obedience will be pleasing to Him.

Anyway, Samuel was not unaware. Once Saul told him that he had carried out God's instructions, Samuel must have quietly looked around and then asked, "What is that I hear? I don't recall you having all these animals before. Where did they come from?" Saul must have realized he was found out, and he started the blame game. I can almost hear him saying, "Oh, those animals? My soldiers did that. I told them not to, but they would not listen." This is a pretty lame excuse. How many soldiers do not follow the orders of the commanding officer? Samuel would have nothing of it. He told Saul what the Lord told him and he ended with a question to Saul, "Why did you disobey?" One day we will be standing before God. Is it possible that God may ask us the same question? Saul must now know he is in big trouble, but he does attempt a response.

1 Samuel 15: 20-21 [20] **"But I did obey the LORD,"** Saul said. "I went on the mission the LORD assigned me. I completely destroyed the Amalekites and brought back Agag their king. [21] The soldiers took sheep and cattle from the plunder, the best of what was devoted to God, in order to sacrifice them to the LORD your God at Gilgal."

Oh Saul, you are making things worse for yourself. Take responsibility for the wrong and fix it. Don't make the hole you have dug for yourself deeper with vain excuses. Saul tried hard to talk his way out of this problem. However, it was too late. Samuel replied to Saul's defense with a message we all need to hear.

1 Samuel 15: 22-23 [22] But Samuel replied: "Does the LORD delight in burnt offerings and sacrifices as much as in obeying the voice of the LORD? **To obey is better than sacrifice**, and to heed is better than the fat of rams.
[23] For **rebellion is like the sin of divination**, and **arrogance like the evil of idolatry**. Because you have rejected the word of the LORD, **he has rejected you as king.**"

God rejected Saul because he rejected God's instruction. Even if we give Saul the benefit of the doubt and say he actually believed what he was telling Samuel, the result of his fate is not changed. Maybe he was truly sincere and was planning to offer the best animals to God as a sacrifice. However, Samuel clearly says that obedience is better than sacrifice. Saul's heart had become disengaged from God. No longer did he feel the need to completely follow the word of God. His actions became self-motivated rather than God-motivated and for that he lost everything. Utter dependence on God means absolute obedience to Him.

Only the Best
In the last section, we saw that Saul tried to convince Samuel that he saved the best animals to give them to God in the form of a sacrifice. This comment was a nice effort on Saul's part to justify his actions. He was trying to cover up a major wrong with a little right. He was trying to use a commonly known fact in Old Testament times concerning sacrifice, that being that God expects only the best. So what does it mean to give God "only the best?" The nice thing about this question is that God Himself provides us with the answer. All through the Bible we can find examples of God telling His children what He expects. We will look at these Biblical examples and use them to determine what He expects from us today.

Old Testament - Gifts to God
In order to understand what it means to give God "only the best," we need to look into the Old Testament. There, God was very particular about what He

liked. In over 50 places we can read where the Lord spoke to Moses. In many of these conversations, as recorded in the book of Leviticus, God was telling Moses what He liked and did not like.

Offering Defined

Offerings are detailed in many of the Lord's instructions. In order to better understand the significance of these offerings, the word "offering" itself needs to be examined. The word "offering" is translated from the Greek word "Corbin" and literally means "bring" or "gift." When we see that an offering to God is actually a gift brought to God, we can then begin to understand what giving "only the best" to God actually means. In the New Testament, Mark uses this word and then goes on to define it as "gift" in Mark 7:11,'Whatever help you might otherwise have received from me is **Corban**' (that is, **gift devoted to God**)

The book of Leviticus goes into great detail concerning the offerings that God expected of His children. These offerings had direction, purpose, and significance. God left nothing to chance and provided offering instructions based on: occasion, emotion, problem, or sin. If the Israelites were happy, they had an offering ready. If they sinned, they had an offering ready. If they needed help, they had an offering ready. The other point of interest is the order of the offerings. When more than one kind of offering was needed, as in Numbers 6:16-17, the order was not random. The prescribed order helps define the importance of the sacrifices as they are given to God.

1. Sin had to be resolved with the sin and guilt offerings. These offerings were mandatory. They were not optional.
2. The worshiper committed himself completely to God with the burnt and grain offerings.
3. Fellowship or communion between the Lord, the priest, and the worshiper was established with the fellowship offering.

These steps were not arbitrary. The worshipper could not fellowship with God until his sins were taken care of and not before he had shown God his devotion. When I read this summary and order given to the Old Testament offerings, the following New Testament passage came to mind:

Matthew 5:23-24 [23]"Therefore, if you are offering your gift at the altar and there remember that your brother has something against you, [24]leave your gift there in front of the altar. First go and be reconciled to your brother; then come and offer your gift.

Perfect Offerings

Offerings were a huge part of life to an Israelite. God expected effort and accuracy in order for an offering to be acceptable to Him. As we read through Leviticus with an eye on offerings, there is a phrase pertaining to sacrifice that keeps showing up. That phrase is "without defect" and "proper value." Not only did each action have an offering associated with it, the offering had to be perfect. In other words, if an offering required a goat, the goat had to be perfect. Not only does the offering of an animal need to be perfect, but it must also have the proper value based on a defined monetary standard. Why do you think the Lord required a perfect specimen? The message that God is trying to convey is that there is a strong consequence to sin and that consequence has to hurt. God is also letting his children know that He is worthy of the absolute best they have to offer. We also see that God is not a tyrant. He proportions sacrifices based on the income of the person. God does not ask for more than we can give.

The short overview of the purpose of Old Testament offerings helped me better appreciate other verses related to offerings and gifts to God. For example:

1 Chronicles 16:28-30 [28]Ascribe to the Lord, O families of nations, ascribe to the Lord glory and strength, [29]ascribe to the Lord the glory due his name. **Bring an offering** and come before him; worship the Lord in the splendor of his holiness. [30]Tremble before him, all the earth!

In this passage we see that the worshipers are to bring a gift to God. We also start to see the attitude of these worshipers. They depend on God, they are humbled by his greatness, and they are in awe of his power.

Deuteronomy 26:10 "And now I bring the **first fruits** of the soil that you, O Lord, have given me." Place the basket before the Lord your God and bow down before him.

In this passage we see that the first fruits of the land were given to God. Not the OK fruits, or the ones no one wanted, but the first fruits. God deserves the best and we should be glad to give Him the best.

Did Not Take Long

The sacrifice system was put in place to help keep the Israelites focused on God's power. However, before the formal offering system was even put in place, we read of sacrifices that were not pleasing to God. In fact, the first recorded sin has to do with a sacrifice that God did not accept. We can read about this in Genesis, chapter 4:2-8. In this passage, Cain gave some of his goods to the Lord while Abel gave the firstborn of his flock to the Lord. The Lord liked Abel's gift, but He was not pleased with Cain's gift. He let Cain know of his disappointment. Rather than Cain doing the right thing, he killed his brother. Cain messed up, but what we see in this passage is that God will not accept just any old offering. Even then, he expected the best. This example of Cain's poor choice is the first example of a poor sacrifice. However, there are several other examples. In fact, in the last book of the Old Testament, we can see that the Lord got quite upset about the quality of the gifts He had been getting.

Blemished Sacrifices

Time has a way of softening the requirements. I can imagine that over the 1,000 years following Moses' instructions, people started trying to change the specifics of the offerings. I can almost hear them talking about why it should be OK to not sacrifice the best animal, but the animal that was expendable. "After all, the best animal cost money and surely God would want me to have money. So, I just can't see how God will care all that much if I offer this goat with a limp." This little talk may seem funny, but from the looks of the passage in Malachi, this type of "rule" changing was taking place. God finally had enough and let his people know. Malachi 1:6-12 indicates that people were making changes to the requirements related to the offerings. In fact, the changes had become so commonplace that the people giving the offerings could not understand why the Lord was upset.

> Malachi 1: 7 "You place defiled food on my altar." But you ask, 'How have we defiled you?' "By saying that the LORD's table is contemptible. [8] When you bring blind animals for sacrifice, is that not wrong? When you sacrifice crippled or diseased animals, is that not wrong? **Try offering them to your governor! Would he be pleased with you? Would he accept you?"** says the LORD Almighty.

This passage shows a God that is very unhappy about His people offering him lame, blind, and diseased animals. How far from right could they have been? Not only did God give his people detailed standards to follow, He warned them not to offer these types of blemished animals.

> Deuteronomy 15:21 If an animal has a defect, is lame or blind, or has any serious flaw, you must **not** sacrifice it to the Lord your God.

Could God have been clearer in this passage? Yet as we said earlier, time and apathy have a way of softening the rules. People were so sure they were in the right that they could not understand how the Lord had been defiled. Here are two questions that come to mind:

1. How long does someone have to do something wrong before they accept that act as right?
2. How clever is Satan to make wrong seem right?

We must realize that wrong never transforms into right, no matter what the time frame. Sinful acts that become the norm take years of small, nearly imperceptible changes. No matter how much time went by, no matter how much self-assurance they had, no matter how sincere they were, no matter what their position in the community, they were still wrong. If a nation could be led astray, why can't we also? If we don't take time to examine the Scriptures to determine if our worship is acceptable before God, we will fall in to the same trap as these priests. There is a right and good way, and we have to find it. One of the clues for following God's commands is best said by Jeremiah.

> Jeremiah 6:16 This is what the Lord says: "Stand at the crossroads and look; ask for the ancient paths, ask where the good way is, and walk in it, and you will find rest for your souls."

Modern Day – Gifts to God

"Person" of God

The Old Testament is rich with color concerning the "person" of God. We see that God could be grieved, be made upset, and be happy. We also see that God expected devotion and dedication from His chosen people. He also knew His children would not always measure up to His standards or expectations. As a loving Father, He had to be strict but loving, firm but understanding. He was laying down a foundation for future generations of Christians to follow and we get to read those struggles in the Old Testament.

Parents and Children

In a very real sense, the way a parent takes care of the needs of a child is the same as the way God took care of His chosen people. An infant derives knowledge from experience as well as the direction of the parent. The parent has to teach the infant how to recognize danger, what not to touch, and so on. If you are a parent, how often did you have to tell your child not to do something? I was always telling my kids to be careful. However they often made mistakes and those mistakes sometimes taught them the biggest lessons. God's children had been living a life of oppression for hundreds of years when He rescued them from Egypt. They knew very little of the ways of the Lord. So the Lord had to tell them everything. He had to tell them how to crawl, how to walk, what not to touch, how to act, and so on. As a parent, the job of raising my children has been both extremely rewarding as well as undeniably difficult. The highs and lows of being a parent parallel the highs and lows of the Old Testament concerning God and His children. However, at some point the child grows up. As I see my children growing, I find I don't have to warn them of danger as much as I used to. Now they can recognize danger and do a good job of avoiding it.

At some point, the child matures and hopefully follows the road laid down for them. The Bible even talks about this in the following passage:

Proverbs 22:6 Train a child in the way he should go, and when he is old he will not turn from it.

Is it possible that the Old Testament is the recorded history of a Father raising His children? Have you ever had a bully pick on your child? I have and I can tell you I was breathing fire. I confronted the kid, the parent, and a few others in order to resolve the problem. Could this be why God got so upset with the Amalekites? The Amalekites had bullied His kids. So God promised to remove them from the face of the earth.

The rules of the Old Testament seem strange, demanding, and even unrealistic, but perhaps no stranger than us telling our children not to touch the stove or not to play in the street. However, if the rules we apply to our children were applied to us as adults, they would also seem strange, demanding, and unrealistic. When was the last time you were told not to play in the street, to chew your food, to take a nap, or to not run with scissors? The people of the Old Testament needed direction and God gave it to them, but what about today? Is it possible that God has already trained His children in the way they should go? Is it possible that His children are now grown? Is it possible that today we are His adult children? I think the possibility of all these questions having a yes answer is pretty good.

Adult Children
How does your relationship with your parents change as we go from infant to teen to adult? I look at the relationship I have with my parents. I can't tell you the last time my parents disciplined me. When I was a child, I did what my parents told me because I had to. If I did not, my Dad could whip off his belt pretty fast. He was also good with a ping-pong paddle. I can recall my sister and I having to go to the basement and pick out the ping-pong paddle we were going to get spanked with. We had a choice of sand paper or rubber. We always picked rubber, thinking that would hurt less. However, it did not matter much - the discipline made its point. Now that I am an adult, I do what my parents want me to because I love them, honor them, and I still want them to be proud of me. Today my relationship with my parents is guided with my heart rather than with a ping-pong paddle.

In the Old Testament, we see that God governed His children with strict discipline. In contrast, the New Testament shows a relationship with the Father that is governed by the attitude of the heart. This reference to the heart can be seen in the following passage:

Luke 16:15 He said to them, "You are the ones who justify yourselves in the eyes of men, but **God knows your hearts**. What is highly valued among men is detestable in God's sight.

I have heard people say that God wrote the New Testament because He made a mistake with the Old Testament laws. That is not true. God does not make mistakes. His Old Testament laws were absolutely needed and just. If we were not given the Old Testament, we would have:

- No record of how God taught and disciplined His children.
- No examples of the "person" of God.
- No idea of what God expects in regards to gifts.

When we look at the Bible as a giant parenting handbook, we see that the Old Testament Israelites were the infants, the New Testament first-century Christians were the teenagers, and today's modern day Christians are the adults. All of us throughout history who follow in His ways are referred to as God's children.

Today we honor God because we love Him, not because we will get disciplined if we don't. Does this mean that God has become softer? Does this mean that God no longer expects gifts? Does this mean that God no longer expects perfection? No, God still expects gifts from His children, but the type of gift is much different than the examples we read of in the Old Testament. The gifts we read of in the New Testament are related to our heart.

Living Sacrifice

The gift we are required to give God today takes much more effort and time than the gifts of the Old Testament. The gifts today involve our life. We read this in Romans 12:1. In the Old Testament, we read about the demanding requirements of the offerings God expected. We saw that God demanded offerings for every occasion. The offerings not only had to be perfect, they had to be of the proper value. These offerings were intended to be a constant reminder to His children that God was in charge, present, and in control. In the New Testament, God gave us His son as the perfect sacrifice. Christ's death on the cross was the ultimate and last physical sacrifice. Christ's death does not mean we no longer are responsible for bringing gifts to God. Rather, Christ's death made it possible to move from a physical sacrifice to a living one, us. God now expects His adult children to live a life constantly aware of His presence. That awareness changes our heart (Acts 11:23, Luke 6:45). When the heart is aligned with God, then we naturally will try to search out the ways to make Him happy. I find the passage in Matthew 25:31-46 concerning the judgment quite interesting when talking about giving God only the best. I am no farmer, buy I can tell the difference between a sheep and a goat. Those that will get to go to heaven will be placed on the right and are classified as sheep. The Lord is bragging on the sheep telling them that they had taken care of Him under all kinds of adverse situations. Now, if I were one of the sheep in this example, I am not sure I would try to talk God out of His praise of me. However, the sheep have to ask the question, "When did we see you in these adverse situations?" The Lord must have smiled as he told them they had taken care of Him when they took care of others. The sheep have such a heart aligned with Christ and are so dedicated to being a living sacrifice, that good works become as natural as breathing. They no longer had to think about doing good works. They just did them naturally.

On the contrary, the goats were quite surprised to hear their fate. They wanted examples of when they had not taken care of the Lord. The Lord basically tells them they are a cursed group and sends them off to eternal destruction. What had these people done wrong? In short, God did not accept their living sacrifice because their heart was not right. They did not strive to walk in His ways. For if they had, they would not have just walked on by when they saw someone in need. Being an acceptable living sacrifice to God requires that we know Christ, walk in His ways, and allow our heart to be touched by His greatness. As we grow to appreciate the magnitude of Christ, not only will our worship to Him improve, but also our life.

Closing Comments
Fire - In Leviticus 6:13 there is one additional requirement concerning the burnt offering, "The fire must be kept burning on the altar continuously; it must not go out." For this offering, the fire was to be kept burning all the time. The fire acted as a reminder to the people that sin was present in the camp and that the people needed God. The fire was to be a constant reminder to help God's children remain faithful.

Light - Today, we see that we are that fire that is never to go out. In Matthew 5:14, "You are the light of the world. A city on a hill cannot be hidden. [15]Neither do people light a lamp and put it under a bowl." We are the light to the world. When we live our life as a living sacrifice to God, we will be a light to the dark, a reminder of God's presence to the world, and be constantly reminded that sin is everywhere. The source of our light is the realization that God is real and Christ is our savior.

Worship
The worship of God is something that goes on every day, not just on Sunday. A living sacrifice does not spring to life on Sunday and die on Monday. We are a living sacrifice that when coupled with Christ results in a perfect gift that we can give to God on every occasion. When we come together to worship God, we must have a heart of worship that is aware of God's greatness, humbled by His

power, in awe of His brilliance, filled with a sense of wonder, thrilled to be in His presence, dedicated to His instructions, and completely dependent on Him. This heart of worship is the gift God deserves and defines the phrase "Kiss toward" God.

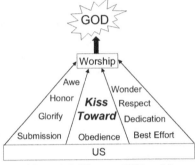

Figure 5: Heart of Worship

The following is a quote from Wayne Jackson. "Finally, as we determine the course of "true worship," let us worship with **great passion**. We must not convey to the world the impression that the worship of our God is a boring, lifeless ritual. We have been redeemed from sin. Let us therefore praise our Maker as those who are grateful for His bountiful blessings. "

His wise words sum up our goal. **The Church that Christ Built** is dedicated to being a light to the world and developing the appropriate heart of a Christian.

Questions to Consider
1. What can we do that shows we utterly depend on God?
2. Does God take unauthorized rule changes lightly?
3. What are examples of God being a Father figure to His chosen people of the Old Testament?
4. Out of the overflow of what, does the mouth speak? How is this filled?
5. What does your worship service do to enforce the proper mind of Christ?
6. What are ways we can submit to the Lord?
7. If we are not to worry, are we not to be concerned? Does the lack of worry mean a free and carefree spirit?
8. What statement makes sense? I did not get anything out of Church today! Or Did God get anything out of Church today?

Chapter 6: Church Defined

My Church

The chapters leading up to this point in the book have paved the way for what lies ahead. Our hard work is about to pay off, and in this chapter, we finally get to see **the Church that Christ Built**.

Mine

When you hear the word "mine" what do you think of? My first thought is of a toddler with a toy, but not any toy - a toy that another child wants. The two children have not quite got sharing figured out and a little squabble breaks out. During the squabble, the phrase most often heard is, "Mine, mine, mine." This may be childish, but how is it different than when I introduce my family, or my wife, or my son, or my daughter to a group of people? The term "mine" implies ownership. When someone says, "This is mine," that phrase necessarily means, "That is not yours." Beyond ownership, the term "mine" often implies pride. I am proud to introduce my family as mine. Sometimes we say things like, "My degree is from such and such," or "My car looks great," or "My house has so many square feet." The number of examples is endless. No matter how many times I hear someone say something is his or hers, I respect that "something" because it is important to him or her. They feel a sense of responsibility, ownership, and pride related to the item they are claiming as their own. The same is true when the phrase is used in the Bible. In Matthew, Christ makes the first announcement that He is about to start building.

> Matthew 16:18 And I tell you that you are Peter, and on this rock **I will build my Church**, and the gates of Hades will not overcome it."

The fact that He uses the term "my" implies a project that is very near and dear to Christ's heart. If this project was not important to Christ, He may have used a term like "a Church" rather than "my Church." This is where we see the excitement in the eyes of Christ, the ultimate builder. Our job is to figure out what Christ was about to build and why what He was about to build was so important that He called it His.

Building Definitions

As we read through the New Testament, we see that what Christ calls Church actually has three parts. The understanding of these parts is important to capture the essence and power of what Christ is about to build. Those terms are:

The Church	Colossians 1:18, 24
The Body of Christ	Ephesians 1:22, 23
The Kingdom	Acts 8:12

As a point of interest, the word "church" appears 79 times in the New Testament, and the word "churches" appears 35 times. The word "kingdom" appears 152 times in the New Testament, and "kingdoms" is found 3 times.

The Term Church

The word "church" was translated from the Greek word "ekklesia." The definition of ekklesia is assembly. In Bible times, the term ekklesia was a common word for describing a group of people. Surely Christ was building something more than an assembly of people? We will see that God has the ability to change anything He wants. In this case, He takes a common word and builds on that word. If we look at a few references in the Bible where the word "church" is used, we start to see why Christ picked this common word.

Ekklesia

Assembly used in the Bible generally refers to a group of people who have been called together for any purpose.

- Acts 19:32 The **assembly** was in confusion: Some were shouting one thing, some another. Most of the people did not even know why they were there.
- Acts 19:39-41 [39]If there is anything further you want to bring up, it must be settled in a legal **assembly**. . . . [41]After he had said this, he dismissed the **assembly**.

In this example, a riot was about to break out. Paul describes the group of people who were in confusion as an ekklesia or assembly. He goes on to describe a legal setting that would be needed to solve this problem and also uses the same word, assembly. He then dismissed the group of people with the same word assembly. In all three cases, the term "assembly" came from the Greek word ekklesia. I have heard it said that if a farmer had a herd of cattle and the cattle were all congregating in an area of the field, the farmer would have referred to the herd as an ekklesia gathering together.

Assembly of Believers

In the following passages, we see that the term "church" refers not just to any assembly of people, but rather to an assembly of people who believe in Christ. The term "church" is used to describe people who come together for the specific purpose of worshiping God. In particular, we see church being used to describe assemblies of believers in the following ways: Compositional, Local, and Regional.

- Romans 16:3-5 [3]Greet Priscilla and Aquila, my fellow workers in Christ Jesus. [4]They risked their lives for me. Not only I but all the churches of the **Gentiles** are grateful to them. [5]Greet also the church that meets at **their house**. Greet my dear friend Epenetus, who was the first convert to Christ in the **province of Asia**.

- Galatians 1:2 To the churches in **Galatia**:
- Acts 9:31 Then the church throughout **Judea, Galilee and Samaria** enjoyed a time of peace. It was strengthened; and encouraged by the Holy Spirit, it grew in numbers, living in the fear of the Lord.
- 1 Corinthians 1:2 To the church of God in **Corinth, to those sanctified in Christ Jesus** and called to be holy, together with all **those everywhere** who **call on the name of our Lord** Jesus Christ—their Lord and ours.
- 1 Corinthians 11:18 In the first place, I hear that when you come together as a **church**, there are divisions among you, and to some extent I believe it.

These references show us that Christ built something called a church that is made up of a group of people who believe in God. This group is not exclusive, but inclusive to anyone who strives to walk in the ways of the Lord.

The Body of Christ

The fact that Christ built something that can be described as an assembly of believers is nice, but hardly earth shattering. In fact, if what Christ built stopped here, His church would be nothing more than a neat social club. Christ built so much more than that, the next few passages give us a much better view of what Christ built.

- Colossians 1:18 And **he is the head of the body, the church**; he is the beginning and the firstborn from among the dead, so that in everything he might have the supremacy.
- Colossians 1: 24 Now I rejoice in what was suffered for you, and I fill up in my flesh what is still lacking in regard to Christ's afflictions, for the sake of **his body, which is the church**.
- Ephesians 1:22-23 [22]And God placed all things under his feet and appointed him to be **head over everything for the church,** [23]**which is his body**, the fullness of him who fills everything in every way.
- Ephesians 5:23 For the husband is the head of the wife as **Christ is the head of the church, his body, of which he is the Savior.**

These passages use the mental imagery of a head and a body. The head contains the brains and directs the affairs of the body. When was the last time you had to scold your foot for walking in a different direction or tell your stomach to digest some food? You never have to do that. Your brain takes care of the affairs of the body. Everyone who has a head can relate to these examples. God uses these examples to explain the relationship between Christ and His church. These passages tell us that Christ is, without question, the head of His body. That is no surprise; I am the head of my body. However, in my case my body is me. In Christ's case, His body is the assembly of believers.

Christ built an institution that allows the world to "see" Him in the flesh. In a very real way, the church is an ambassador of Christ to the world. Have you ever stopped to realize that as a Christian, we may be the closest thing to Christ some people will ever see? What impression are you leaving?

The Kingdom of God

The term "kingdom of God" or "kingdom of Heaven" is used several times in reference to **the Church that Christ Built**. The implication is that **the Church that Christ Built** is not only an assembly of believers, or merely a reflection of the body of Christ, but also an earthly representation of Heaven. The following passages provide insight into this aspect of Christ's church.

- Acts 8:12 But when they believed Philip as he preached the good news of the **kingdom of God** and the name of Jesus Christ, they were baptized, both men and women.
- Luke 1:31-33 And behold, you will conceive in your womb, and bear a son, and you shall name Him Jesus. He will be great, and will be called the Son of the Most High; and the Lord God will give Him the throne of His father David; and He will reign over the house of Jacob forever, and His **kingdom will have no end**.
- Matt 11:11 I tell you the truth: Among those born of women there has not risen anyone greater than John the Baptist; yet he who is least in the **kingdom of heaven** is greater than he.
- John 3:5 Jesus answered, "I tell you the truth, no one can enter the **kingdom of God** unless he is born of water and the Spirit.
- Colossians 1:13 For he has rescued us from the dominion of darkness and brought us into the **kingdom** of the Son he loves, [14]in whom we have redemption, the forgiveness of sins.
- Luke 17: 20-21 [20]Once, having been asked by the Pharisees when the kingdom of God would come, Jesus replied, "The kingdom of God does not come with your careful observation, [21]nor will people say, 'Here it is,' or 'There it is,' because the **kingdom of God is within** (or among) **you**."

These passages lead us to a better understanding of what kingdom means. God uses the earthly definition of kingdom to describe what Christians inherit. The similarities are that the people of a kingdom are subject to their king, the difference being that the kingdom of God is a spiritual kingdom rather than a physical one. The kingdom of God represents those who have taken on the name of Christ. Those in the kingdom will inherit eternal life with the Father.

When we look at **the Church that Christ Built**, we see pure genius. Christ knows how forgetful we as humans can be. We have to have something to remember Him by. Christ knows that if we will just follow Him, many of our problems would disappear. So He developed a system to help us get to heaven.

His plan involves the creation of a church that is the reflection of Heaven on earth. It is an assembly of believers, the body of Christ, and is under the care and direction of Christ Himself!

Putting these pieces together allows us to see that the church allows Christ to do His work. In so doing, Christians become the closest representative of God that some people will ever see. The magnitude of what Christ built is unprecedented. He used a common word that represented any old assembly and converted it into a word that represents a spiritual institution. When we realize the power of what Christ has done, then going to church becomes a blessing rather than a chore. We should be looking forward to being in the assembly of believers because we represent Christ. We need to realize that we are held to a higher standard because we are heirs of a prestigious kingdom, the kingdom of God.

I have been guilty of getting up on Sunday and not feeling like going to church. However, as I learn more about what Christ built, those feelings have faded. When I hear people say they don't go to church or they don't feel the need to go to church, that tells me they haven't learned to appreciate the magnitude of what Christ has built. Maybe their image of church is more like a social club, one where you pay the membership dues and you get to be a member. However, that view misses the mark of what Christ built. As I learn more about what Christ has built, the passage in Hebrews becomes more real to me.

> Hebrews 12: 28-29 [28]Therefore, since we are **receiving a kingdom** that cannot be shaken, let us **be thankful**, and so **worship God acceptably with reverence and awe**, [29]for our "God is a consuming fire."

We have been given a gift more valuable than we can comprehend. We need to be thankful for that gift, and worship our Father in heaven in an acceptable fashion with reverence and awe. Going to church does not mean going to a building. Nowhere in Scripture do we see that **the Church that Christ built** is a physical building. The church is the assembly of believers. The church is not something that you go in and out of, it is not a building, it is something that we are part of, the body of Christ. Wow!!!

A Word about Order

The church is made up of a group of people. In order for that group of people to have their hearts and minds directed toward God, God gives us instructions on how this assembly is to behave. One of the most compelling examples of conduct during our meeting together is found in the following passage.

> 1 Corinthians 14:40 But everything should be done in a **fitting and orderly way**.

This passage is at the end of a long list of instructions that is being given to the Corinthians. At the end of these instructions, the term "fitting and orderly way" is used. When viewed from other translations, this verse begins to give us insights into what is meant by this phrase.

- Let all things be done decently and in order.
- Let all things be done in an "appropriate" and "becoming" manner; "decorously," as becomes the worship of God.
- Let all be done in "order, regularly;" without confusion or discord.

The Greek phrase used for these translations is kata taxin. This Greek word is normally used as a military term that denotes the order and regularity with which an army is drawn up. The adverb "properly" literally means "of good external appearance." The term "In order" can be defined as: "Due or right order." Literally, order, i.e., a fixed succession observing also a fixed time. When these terms are put together, we can read that the assembly of believers needs to reflect official dignity.

When we realize we are worshipping God, the phrase "fitting and orderly way" has significance. Just take a look in Revelation 5:9-14 when John watches a worship service. John was given a "peek under the tent" concerning Heaven. What he saw was beyond his ability to put into words. He was amazed at the worship of God that he was witnessing. We are talking about the worship of God. He expects an assembly of believers to worship Him in a fitting and orderly manner. A "fitting and orderly" worship is not to say that worship has to be boring. On the contrary, when we realize we are worshipping God, we should have an unbelievable sense of awe and wonder come over us. The assembly of believers is far from boring, at least in **the Church that Christ Built**.

The Rock

The foundation of a building is crucial to the stability of that structure. The same must be true of the institution that Christ built. In order for this institution to stand, a foundation worthy of this structure is required. We need to look into this foundation to better understand that Christ did not just come up with this church idea on a whim. He spent a considerable amount of time making sure the foundation was in place before starting to build. In Ephesians 2:19-21 we see just how solid the foundation is.

> [19]Consequently, you are no longer foreigners and aliens, but **fellow citizens** with God's people and members of God's household, [20]built on the **foundation** of the **apostles** and **prophets,** with **Christ Jesus himself as the chief cornerstone**. [21]In him the whole building is joined together and rises to become a holy temple in the Lord.

Family

I want to share a story before getting into the talk about the foundation. Verse 19 makes reference to fellow citizens and members of God's household and reminds me of an opportunity I was given when I did a job in France. My daughter was only 6 months old and I was about to go to Lyon for three weeks. Not a long stay, but long enough that my work allowed me to take my wife and daughter. In preparation for the trip, we happened to find missionaries in the town where we were going to stay. When Sunday rolled around, we went to the address we had for the Church. We drove up to the building and waited. Then we waited some more, and then some more. We finally realized that no one was showing up. What a terrible feeling fell over Kim and I. We had the uncomfortable feeling that the church had died and that we may be the only "Christ" these people will ever see. What a humbling and lonely feeling. As it turns out, they had outgrown that small building and had relocated. After a few phone calls, we found them. We gave them a call and were relieved to hear English. If you have ever been to a foreign country, you really starve just to hear a familiar language. The missionaries (Pam and Charles) invited Kim and my daughter to spend the day with them while I was at work. This was a welcome gesture since Kim had been locked up in a hotel for a week. On the first day with them, Kim and Kayla were playing on the floor with Pam. Charles and Pam had just moved into this house and were having some work done. One of the contractors noticed my wife and daughter playing on the floor with Pam and asked Pam who these people were. Pam told them they were friends of theirs from the States. The contractor then asked how long they had known each other. Pam told them we met last night. The contractor's mouth hit the ground; He could not believe that perfect strangers were playing in their house. Pam told them we were Christians and that was the kind of thing Christians do. She is right.

When we put on the name of Christ, we have a family who wraps around the world. This is a gift that we do not take advantage of nearly enough.

Foundation

Now we get into the second part of the passage in Ephesians. This part deals with the foundation of Christ's church.

> Ephesians 2:20-21 [19]Consequently, you are no longer foreigners and aliens, but fellow citizens with God's people and members of God's household, [20]built on the **foundation** of the **apostles** and **prophets**, with **Christ Jesus himself as the chief cornerstone.** [21]In him the whole building is joined together and rises to become a holy temple in the Lord.

The Church that Christ Built has a foundation that has stood the test of time. The foundation was based on the predictions of the prophets, the teachings of the apostles, and Jesus Christ himself. This three-piece foundation sets the stage for what Christ built. The fact that Christ is the cornerstone is no mistake. The building's cornerstone sets the direction of the entire structure. If the cornerstone is not positioned correctly, then the entire building can end up in the wrong direction. This imagery should not be a big surprise to us. After all, Jesus grew up around carpentry and probably had dealings with building physical structures. The Bible tells us in the following passage that the religious leaders of that day did not follow Jesus' message. In fact, they killed Him. However, Christ's message became the primary element in the development of His church. Matthew 21:42 "The stone the builders rejected has become the cornerstone."

When we look at the prophets, the apostles, and Christ as three parts of the foundation, we see that there is one common ingredient. That ingredient can be found in the following passage in Matthew.

> Matthew 16:15 [15]"But what about you? (Peter)". "Who do you say I am?" [16]Simon Peter answered, "**You are the Christ, the Son of the living God.**" [17]Jesus Replied, "Blessed are you, Simon son of Jonah, for this was not revealed to you by man, but by my Father in heaven. [18]And I tell you that you are **Peter**, an on **this rock I will build my Church**, and the gates of Hades will not overcome it. [19]I will give you the keys of the kingdom of heaven; whatever you bind on earth will be bound in heaven, and whatever you loose on earth will be loosed in heaven."

The term "this rock" is what Christ uses to show the stability of the foundation. We see the term rock used in Matthew 7:24-27 referring to a firm foundation. In this passage, we read of a wise man who built his house upon the rock. We see that wise people build their homes on rock, not sand. The rock represents the words of Jesus, but not just the words - the words of Jesus put into practice. The definition of "the Rock" is clear. However, in Matthew 16:18, the definition of the Rock has generated extreme controversy. In fact, entire religious groups have been formed based on two very different interpretations of the phrase "this rock." One interpretation says that Peter is the rock that Christ is talking about. Those who believe Peter is the rock will use verse 19 to back up their claim. They believe Christ is giving Peter the authority to do whatever he wants. After all, when someone is given the "Keys to a city," that primarily means they have free passage. Christ gave Peter not just the keys to a city, but also the keys to the Kingdom of Heaven.

The other view is Peter's answer in verse 16, "You are the Christ, the Son of the living God" is the rock Christ is talking about. So which interpretation is correct? First, we cannot forget that **the Church that Christ Built** is a gigantic institution. Something this big has to have a firm foundation. One way to help unravel this interpretation problem is to look at the Greek words for Peter and Rock.

The Greek word for Peter, Petros, means a stone or pebble and the Greek word for Rock, Petra, means a ledge of stone. I find it difficult to understand why Christ would choose to build his foundation on a pebble. The visual imagery of a ledge of stone is getting closer to a foundation that has to be strong enough to hold Christ's church. Next, we need to look at the cornerstone of this foundation. The cornerstone is the stone the builders rejected, Christ. Why is Christ so special? Maybe this is obvious, but He is the Son of God. No one else can say that, only Christ. In fact, 1 Corinthians even tells us that no one other than Christ can lay the foundation for His church.

1 Corinthians 3:11 No one can lay any foundation other than the one already laid, which is Jesus Christ.

The two passages that use rock as a reference to a foundation have to agree. In Matthew 7:24, we see that the rock is the active usage of Christ's words. This definition of rock makes it hard to see how a person, Peter, can be the rock in Matthew 16:17. However, if the rock in Matthew 16:17 refers to the fact that Jesus is the Son of God, then the definitions of rock in both passages line up. This is also consistent with Old Testament passages that use Lord and Rock interchangeably.

Psalm 28:1 Of David. To you, **LORD, I call; you are my Rock** . . .

Finally, the foundation for **the Church that Christ built** cannot fail. Christ knows humans fail, so placing the burden of Christ's church on Peter is unlikely. However, the words of Christ are truth. In fact, they are the standard that defines how we should live. When we look at the three parts of the foundation: the prophets, the apostles, and Christ - we see that they are all linked by the teachings of Christ. Christ is the Rock, the standard and the ultimate truth. He defines the foundation that holds His awesome masterpiece, His church.

Prophets Predict It

Prophets are people who told God's will to the people of the Old Testament. The Old Testament is full of passages that talk about the coming of Christ's church. Passages like Zechariah 1:16, Isaiah 2:2-3, Micah 4:1-2 tell us that Christ will build a magnificent structure that will first open in Jerusalem.

The next passage tells us when to expect the grand opening. The interesting point to note is that this next passage was written nearly 600 years before Christ established His church. The passage is in Daniel 2 and has to do with a dream that King Nebuchadnezzar had. The dream troubled the King and he wanted an interpretation. A quick overview of this passage is as follows.

- The Rock - Daniel 2:34, 35 [34]While you were watching, **a rock was cut out**, but not by human hands. It struck the statue on its feet of iron and clay and smashed them. ⋯ But the rock that struck the statue became a huge mountain and filled the whole earth.
- The Interpretation - Daniel 2:44 In the time of **those kings**, the God of heaven will **set up a kingdom** that will never be destroyed, nor will it be left to another people. It will crush all those kingdoms and bring them to an end, but it **will itself endure forever**.

The time of those kings is when Christ will set up His church. A look into history tells us the time period when Christ will open His doors.

- Gold head – Nebuchadnezzar – First world empire.
- The arms and the chest of the image represented the Medo-Persian Empire, the second world empire after Babylon.
- The belly and thighs symbolized the Grecian Empire, which was created by Alexander the Great and was the third world empire.
- The final part of the image illustrated the Roman Empire, which was established by Caesar Augustus in 31 B.C. and was the fourth world empire. The Roman Empire came to an end around 476 years after the birth of Christ.
- The Rock not made with human hands is Christ!

Daniel's prediction is remarkably accurate and tells us that Christ's Kingdom will be established between 31BC and 476 AD. The Old Testament is filled with passages written by prophets that talk about the coming of **the Church that Christ built**. These passages bring me comfort and awe. I guess I never appreciated what church was all about. However, after studying this I came to realize that Christ did not just throw together a church at the last minute. His church was planned over 600 years before it opened the doors. I have a hard time planning 5 years from now. However, God had a plan at least 600 years in advance. How much time and thought did Christ have to put into the creation of His church? I am not sure we can even begin to comprehend the planning and development phase of this project. In order for Christ to have spent so much time in the planning stage, His church must be special. If I think of church as just something to do, then I don't have an appreciation or understanding of what Christ built. The church was not thrown together. The prophets foretold the structure, and this is what it means to have part of the foundation based on the prophets.

Apostles Taught It
Christ knew that his physical time on earth would be cut short. So He had to find people He could rely on to make sure His message and His church would be

properly built. Christ is the ultimate teacher and the apostles had three years to learn from the Master Himself. However, Christ told them not only that they were important, but that the Holy Spirit would help them recall the things He had taught them.

- John 14:26 But the Counselor, the Holy Spirit, whom the Father will send in my name, will teach you all things and will remind you of everything I have said to you.
- Revelation 21:14 The wall of the city had twelve foundations, and on them were the names of the twelve apostles of the Lamb.

The early church would have had many questions. After all, their entire religious upbringing would be shifted. They would no longer be giving physical sacrifices, but spiritual ones. I think we sometimes give the early Christians a hard time. How would you react if for some reason Thanksgiving or Christmas were outlawed? What would you tend to do when that time of the year rolled around? In a very real sense, all of the religious traditions that the Israelites had developed over hundreds of years were now different. Christ did that. I am sure the early church had questions and needed much direction. The fact that Christ left behind His apostles to help with this transition is again nothing short of genius. The fact that the apostles recorded most of these instructions is again an indication of genius. The New Testament is full of apostle teachings concerning how the church is to work. Their help is what makes up the third part of the foundation of Christ's church.

Christ Knows

The foundation of **the Church that Christ built** is set. The foundation is not growing or changing. Some have tried to say that there are modern-day apostles who are still adding to the foundation of the Church. This view is a dangerous extension of what Christ built. Add-ons to Christ's church are unauthorized. A human add-on is a little like placing an old worn out shack right next to a palace. **The Church that Christ built** is awesome and finished. Any attempt to expand the foundation of Christ's church beyond the predictions of the prophets, the teachings of the apostles, and the words of Christ is unnecessary. We see Paul's instruction to Timothy in regard to the foundation of the church.

2 Timothy 2:19 Nevertheless, **God's solid foundation stands firm**, sealed with this inscription: "**The Lord knows those who are his**," and, "**Everyone who confesses the name of the Lord must turn away from wickedness.**"

After reading this passage, the mental picture that came to mind is the following:

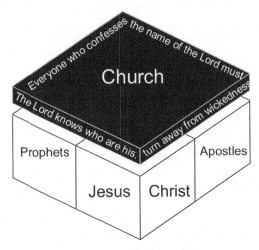

Figure 6: Church Foundation

Christ's church is built on a firm foundation consisting of the prophets, apostles, with Jesus Christ as the cornerstone. The foundation is held together by the living words of Christ, our Rock. The Lord knows who are His. Are you one of them?

Questions to Consider

1. How do you feel about going to church when on vacation or a business trip?
2. What does your church do to hold to the foundation laid out by the prophets, apostles, and Christ?
3. Have you ever relied on a fellow brother or sister for help?
4. What does your church do to promote an atmosphere of "fitting and orderly" worship?

Chapter 7: Grand Opening

Grand Opening

When you hear the phrase, "Grand Opening", what do you think of? I think of balloons, games, and great deals as a business opens its doors for the first time. The business owner is trying to get customers excited about buying something at their store. In the case of **the Church that Christ Built**, we are close to the "grand opening." In this chapter we will look at the events leading up to the opening of the kingdom. It has been said that the greatest story ever told is the story of Jesus Christ. This is very true, but do you know what the second greatest story ever told would be? That story would have to do with the opening of His church.

The Planning Phase

If the amount of planning is proportional to the size of the event, then **the Church that Christ built** must be a big event because the prophets were talking about it hundreds of years before the doors first opened. In Daniel we read about the opening of the kingdom approximately 600 years before the church was officially established.

> Daniel 2:44 In the time of those kings, the God of heaven will set up a **kingdom that will never be destroyed**, nor will it be left to another people. It will crush all those kingdoms and bring them to an end, but it will itself endure forever.

In Zechariah we see that the Lord is planning on having His grand opening in Jerusalem.

> Zechariah 1:16 Therefore, this is what the Lord says: I will return to **Jerusalem** with mercy, and **there my house will be rebuilt**. And the measuring line will be stretched out over Jerusalem, declares the Lord Almighty.

Then in Isaiah and Micah we see again that Jerusalem is the place, but this grand opening will be for something that is mighty.

> Isaiah 2:2-3 (Micah 4:1-2) [2]In the **last days** the **mountain of the Lord's temple** will be established as chief among the mountains; it will be raised above the hills, and all nations will stream to it. [3]Many peoples will come and say, "Come, let us go up to the mountain of the Lord, to the house of the God of Jacob. He will teach us his ways, so that we may walk in his paths." The law will go out from Zion, the word of the Lord from **Jerusalem**.

These passages show us that a mountain is being used to describe the structure Christ is building. A structure that can be compared to a mountain must be tremendous. I have had the opportunity to see several mountains such as the Highlands in Scotland, the Swiss Alps, T-Tons, French Alps, Mount Rainer and Mount St. Helens in Washington, and Mount Hood in Oregon. All of these mountains are nothing short of spectacular. However, as impressive as these mountains are, they are nothing in comparison to Christ's church. What an awesome thought.

The Old Testament is full of predictions related to the time, place, and stature of the structure Christ is building, but with these few passages we can see three things concerning the grand opening of Christ's Church:
1. **Time**: The Church will be established during the Roman Empire. More specifically, Isaiah tells us that the Church will be established in the "Last Days."
2. **Place**: Christ will establish His church in Jerusalem.
3. **Purpose**: God's house is exalted above all others and all nations will flow into it.

The prophets laid the foundation for what Christ is about to open. The fact that Christ was involved 600 years before the grand opening reinforces the significance of what He built. The church did not happen accidently, the church was planned.

Coming Soon

I was driving to the hardware store the other day, and on the way I noticed a new construction project starting. There were bulldozers pushing dirt everywhere, but just out front of the construction there was a large sign that said, "Coming soon . . . ." This told me that the planning had been finished, construction was underway, and that the grand opening was not too far off. The fact that the prophets were talking about the grand opening hundreds of years before the actual event shows that Christ had been planning this event for some time. As we move into the New Testament, there are several clues that can be thought of as a sign that says "Coming soon, **The Church that Christ built.**"

Isaiah 2:2's comparison of Christ's church to a mountain gives us a clue as to when the church is about to start. In the beginning of this passage we read "last days." If we can figure out when the "last days" are, we can get a better idea of when Christ will open the doors. Fortunately, the Hebrews writer makes reference to the time of the last days.

Hebrew 1:1-2 [1]In the past God spoke to our forefathers through the prophets at many times and in various ways, [2]but in **these last days** he has spoken to us by his Son, whom he appointed heir of all things, and through whom he made the universe.

This passage tells us that in the past we received God's words from the prophets, but in "these" last days we hear God's words directly from Christ. This passage not only supports the foundation talked about in Ephesians 2:20 where the church is based on the prophets, Jesus Christ, and the apostles, but it also tells us that the time of the "last days" is during the time of Christ. Digging a little further shows us that the kingdom is just around the corner.

> Matthew 3:1 [1]In those days John the Baptist came, preaching in the Desert of Judea [2]and saying, "Repent, for the **kingdom of heaven is near**." [3]This is he who was spoken of through the prophet Isaiah: "A voice of one calling in the desert, **'Prepare the way for the Lord**, make straight paths for him.' "

This passage refers to John the Baptist and his primary job of preparing the way for the Lord. John was to let people know that Jesus was coming and that the kingdom was near. Keep in mind that the Israelite people had been following the Old Testament laws for generations. Many were expecting an earthly kingdom, not a spiritual one. So the transition to the New Testament was not going to happen overnight. John's job was to start getting the people ready to accept the message Christ was bringing. The next passage is after John the Baptist had been put in prison, but before the apostles had been selected. Notice that Christ is starting to tell people that the kingdom is near.

> Mark 1:15 [14]After John was put in prison, Jesus went into Galilee, proclaiming the good news of God. [15]"The time has come," he said. "**The kingdom of God is near**. Repent and believe the good news!"

The next passages show us that Christ was feeling a sense of urgency to get His message out. He knows that His time on earth is running out. He must have liked how John the Baptist had prepared the people for His message. However, John was now gone and He needed the apostles near Him for instruction. So Christ recruited 72 more people for the primary purpose of going before Him with the message that the kingdom of God is near.

- Luke 10:1-2 [1]After this the Lord **appointed seventy-two others** and sent them two by two ahead of him to every town and place where he was about to go. [2]He told them, "The harvest is plentiful, but the workers are few."
- Luke 10:8-12 [8]"When you enter a town and are welcomed, eat what is set before you. [9]Heal the sick who are there and tell them, **'The kingdom of God is near you**.' [10]But when you enter a town and are not welcomed, go into its streets and say, [11]'Even the dust of your town that sticks to our feet we wipe off against you. Yet be sure of this: **The kingdom of God is near.**' [12]I tell you, it will be more bearable on that day for Sodom than for that town."

These passages tell us that the grand opening is not far off. They also tell us that the message is important to Christ. In fact, He tells the 72 that if people don't like what you are telling them, leave the town and go on. He then says that those who don't want to listen are in for a rough time. If **the Church that Christ built** just happened, why would Christ be working so hard to let people know about it? The answer is that Christ's church did not just happen. Christ built it!

Getting Closer

In the passages leading up to these, we see that the grand opening would be happening soon, but we have not yet nailed down a date. The following passages let us know that the date is going to be within the life span of those who were listening to Christ's message.

- Matthew 16:28 "I tell you the truth, some who are standing here will not taste death before they see the Son of Man coming in his kingdom."
- Mark 9:1 "I tell you the truth, some who are standing here will not taste death before they see the kingdom of God come with power."

These two passages are similar, but the second one gives us more detail as to how the kingdom will come. In the second passage not only will some of the people in the audience see the grand opening, but the grand opening will come with power. We do not yet know what the term "power" means, but when the grand opening happens, we will know it.

Maintenance Crew Getting Ready

The Godhead: the Father, the Son, and the Holy Spirit. What is it? The Bible says that the Godhead is one, but that there are three parts. I have heard this explained by using the analogy of an egg. An egg is an egg, but it has three parts, the shell, the yolk, and the white stuff. I have also heard this explained by looking at a three-leaf clover with each leaf being one of the Godhead. I am not sure we as humans can make sense of the Godhead. These analogies help, but God is God. However, consider the following example of what each member of the Godhead does from the perspective of a job. Suppose that the Father is the master architect and His job is to design everything. The Son is the master builder and His job is to secure the foundation and build His church. That leaves the job of the Holy Spirit. In any building, once the architect and builder are finished, a maintenance crew has to be put in place to make sure the building stands firm. The Holy Spirit represents the maintenance crew. His job is to make sure the plan designed by the Father and set in motion by the Son continues. The following passage has Christ telling His apostles that He must go to make room for the Holy Spirit.

John 16: 5-7 [5] "Now I am going to him who sent me, yet none of you asks me, 'Where are you going?' [6]Because I have said these things, you are filled with grief. [7]But I tell you the truth: It is for your good that I am going away. **Unless I go away, the Counselor will not come to you**; but if I go, I will send him to you."

In Luke we see that during one of Christ's teachings to the apostles, He tells them not to worry about what they are going to say because the Holy Spirit will help them.

Luke 12:11-12 [11]"When you are brought before synagogues, rulers and authorities, do not worry about how you will defend yourselves or what you will say, [12]for the Holy Spirit will teach you at that time what you should say."

The Holy Spirit is referred to as several things in the Bible: Holy Ghost, Holy Spirit, and Counselor. Their Greek source is "paraclete" which literally means the one who walks beside. The Holy Spirit is the one who helps us along the Christian walk. He has a big job. The grand opening must be getting close. Christ is now telling his apostles He has to go. We still are not told when, but the anticipation must be building with the apostles.

Just a few Days Away

The book of Acts starts off when Christ rose from the grave. We see that He stayed around for 40 days and spent most of that time with the apostles letting them know that the kingdom of God was very close. In fact, the grand opening is about to take place within a few days.

Acts 1:3-5 [3]After his suffering, . . . He appeared to them over a period of **forty days** and spoke about the **kingdom of God**. [4]On one occasion, while he was eating with them, he gave them this command: "**Do not leave Jerusalem**, but **wait for the gift** my Father promised, which you have heard me speak about. [5]For John baptized with water, but in a **few days** you will be baptized with the Holy Spirit."

Can you imagine what must have been going through the minds of the apostles? These men had stopped their "normal" line of work nearly three years before and had spent every waking hour with the Son of God. They must have realized they were special for being allowed an awesome experience of being with Christ. They saw Him killed on a cross, yet here they are spending 40 days with Him after He was killed. Christ spends time teaching them about the kingdom of God, and proving to them that He really is Christ and that He is alive. Then, Christ gives them one final command. The command has two parts:
1. Do not leave Jerusalem.
2. Wait for my Father's gift.

Why does Jesus give them this command? He wants them to be around for the grand opening of His church. I almost feel bad for the apostles. They must have been confused. We see in the next passage that the apostles still did not understand.

> Acts 1:6-9 So when they met together, they asked him, "Lord, are you at this time going to restore the kingdom of Israel?" [7]He said to them: "It is not for you to know the times or dates the Father has set by his own authority. [8]But you will receive power when the Holy Spirit comes on you; and you will be my witnesses in Jerusalem, and in all Judea and Samaria, and to the ends of the earth." After he said this, he was taken up before their very eyes, and a cloud hid him from their sight.

They were expecting the Lord to start an earthly kingdom. Christ came back from the dead, spent 40 days teaching them about the spiritual kingdom He was building, and then they ask this question, "When are you going to build your earthly Kingdom?" I can almost see Christ smile as He told them all would be fine as He traveled back home.

I can only begin to imagine the emotion these men were feeling. They were going to receive a gift from God, and it was going to be power. They had to be excited about this gift, but at the same time they had to be sad knowing that Christ, their friend, had just left them. In these passages, we see that the grand opening of **the Church that Christ Built** will happen in a few days, occur in Jerusalem, and start with power. So was anything going on in the next few days in Jerusalem? Christ did not leave anything to chance. You can rest assured that something big was just around the corner. A little thing the Jews called Pentecost.

Doors Opened

Now for the cutting of the ribbon, the grand opening, the unlocking of the doors, the beginning of **the Church that Christ built**! The apostles were told to stay in Jerusalem for a few days. Why was this? Well, the day of Pentecost was about to start. Jerusalem was the place to be if you were an Israelite because Pentecost was a feast of joy and thanksgiving to God for the blessing of their harvest. Pentecost means 50 and it was to be started 50 days after the Passover. An interesting point is that the Pentecost would have started on the first day of the week. The Passover was designed to help the Israelites remember their deliverance from Egyptian bondage. The time of these feasts had to be a big deal in Jerusalem. There must have been people everywhere. Pentecost was probably something like our Thanksgiving. Relatives and friends travel all over the place to be with each other during this time. The difference for the Israelites was that everyone came to Jerusalem. Again, we see the genius of the Lord. Where else to have a grand opening but in a place that was packed?

When the day of Pentecost came, the apostles were all together when the power came. Most likely they were in the temple. We see in Luke that when Christ left them, they went to the temple.

- Luke 23:50-53 [50]When he had led them out to the vicinity of Bethany, he lifted up his hands and blessed them. [51]While he was blessing them, he left them and was taken up into heaven. [52]Then they worshiped him and returned to Jerusalem with great joy. [53]And **they stayed continually at the temple**, praising God.
- Acts 2:1-4 [1]When the **day of Pentecost** came, they were all together in one place. [2]Suddenly a **sound like the blowing of a violent wind** came from heaven and filled the whole house where they were sitting. [3]They saw what seemed to be **tongues of fire** that separated and came to rest on each of them. [4]All of them were filled with the Holy Spirit and began to **speak in other tongues** as the Spirit enabled them.

The grand opening of **the Church that Christ Built** is here! The apostles were together when the heavens opened and a sound like a violent wind fills the building. Can you relate to violent wind? Fortunately, I have not been in a tornado, but just last night we had a major thunderstorm in our area. The tornado siren went off and we had to go to the basement. The sound of the wind and thunder was spectacular. As I was listening, I wondered if these were even close to what the apostles experienced. Here are the apostles in the midst of what sounds like a violent storm. They would have all been looking at each other with fear and anticipation, then they notice that each has what appears to be fire on their heads. If that were me, I would be looking for some water to put the fire out. However, the realization of what was happening must have finally sunk in. All that they had been studying with their friend Jesus was happening - the grand opening of the kingdom of God! The prophecy was fulfilled on that first day of Pentecost when the following things happened:

- The church was established in the time of the Roman Empire.
- The church originated in Jerusalem.
- The church came with power.
- The apostles were given a gift from the Father.

The sound of the wind was not just isolated to that room. In Acts 2:5-13 we read that the commotion must have been great because all of a sudden a crowd of people were looking for the apostles to see what was happening. Remember, Jerusalem would be packed with people at this time. The Israelites hear this sound and flock to see what it is. Try not to look at a car accident next time you pass one. The natural curiosity of the people was too great. They had to find out what the commotion was. As the crowd gathered, they were amazed and confused. The Bible says bewildered. That sums it up pretty well. Why were they bewildered? They were all hearing the apostles speak in the native language of those in the crowd. This was especially strange to the crowd because they knew the apostles did not naturally know this language. The crowd was perplexed wanting to know the meaning of all this. Unfortunately, even the majestic and powerful entry of the Holy Spirit was not enough to convince all those in the crowd. Some made fun of the apostles and even said they were drunk. However, this was just the jab Peter needed.

> Acts 2:14-15 [14]Then **Peter stood up** with the Eleven, raised his voice and addressed the crowd: "Fellow Jews and all of you who live in Jerusalem, let me explain this to you; listen carefully to what I say. [15]**These men are not drunk, as you suppose. It's only nine in the morning!**"

Peter sets the record straight then proceeds to give the first sermon. The grand opening of **the Church that Christ Built** would not be complete without a sermon, and that is what Peter delivered. However, isn't it a little strange that Peter is giving the first sermon? After all, he had betrayed Christ just prior to Christ's crucifixion, but now here he is.

Here are the Keys

There are a few passages that imply Christ knew Peter would be giving the first sermon. Recall the passage in Matthew that talks about Peter and the foundation Christ will use for His church. If we read verse 19, we see that Christ is giving Peter the keys to the kingdom.

> Matthew 16:18-19 [18]And I tell you that you are Peter, and on this rock I will build my church, and the gates of Hades will not overcome it. [19]**I will give you the keys of the kingdom of heaven**; whatever you bind on earth will be bound in heaven, and whatever you loose on earth will be loosed in heaven

This was the first sermon at the grand opening of **the Church that Christ built**. The doors had been shut until this moment. However, when Peter started His sermon, the doors were opened. In a very real sense, his sermon was the key that opened the door. His words were important and binding. We also see a reference in Luke concerning Satan and Peter (also called Simon).

> Luke 22: 31-32 [31]"Simon, Simon, **Satan has asked to sift you as wheat**. [32]But I have prayed for you, Simon, that your faith may not fail. And when you have turned back, strengthen your brothers."

The Lord tells (Simon) Peter that Satan is after him, but that Christ was praying for Peter. He then tells Peter that he will turn back and when he does, he will strengthen his brothers. Well, he did fail during the crucifixion of Christ, but he comes back with power during the grand opening. Is it possible that Satan may have tried to derail Peter? Is it possible that Satan may have been thinking that if he could derail Peter, then maybe the doors of the kingdom would not open? No one knows for sure, but Christ knew and He did not leave anything to chance. Christ knew Peter would be giving the first sermon, and that sermon hit the mark.

Peter tells those in the crowd what was going on. Peter knows his audience and he knows they would have a good understanding of the Old Testament. So he starts with Old Testament predictions of Christ and the establishment of His church. He also builds on their knowledge of David to set the stage for Christ. He goes on to tell them that the person they just killed was the Christ they had been studying about their entire life. Peter let his audience know that they had not only missed Christ, they had killed him. His message hit them like a ton of bricks. When they realized what they had done, they wanted to know how they could fix the problem. They had to know what could be done. Peter tells them what they must do to enter the kingdom: Repent and be baptized. That was enough for at least 3,000 of them because that is how many were added to the kingdom as a result of the first sermon.

The First Sermon

Peter and the other apostles must have been in a near daze as the things Christ told them would happen were actually happening. They all had flames on their heads, they were speaking in foreign tongues, there was the sound of rushing wind, and there were tons of people filtering in. However, we see in verse 15 that Peter snapped to life when the crowd accused them of being drunk. In Acts 2:16-21 He tells them that was not the case and proceeds with the first sermon. The remark about being drunk was the spark that ignited Peter into action. Peter continues his sermon as follows. Peter was talking with Israelites who would have known the Old Testament very well. In fact, they had studied these prophesies since they were old enough to go to Bible school. I have always been impressed with how Peter started his talk. He started his sermon with common ground. Nothing in this passage would have been unknown to his audience. If Peter had started by telling them how wrong they were for having killed the Son of God, I would imagine his sermon would have ended pretty quickly. However, since he started with common ground, he piqued the interest of his audience. He continued in Acts 2:22 to let them know that the person they had been waiting for and studying about for their entire life had just been there. Again we see the wisdom of Peter. He knows many in his audience would have known Jesus. They would have seen the many miracles Christ had performed. Notice that the crowd did not argue with Peter as he told them about Jesus. Then he lets them know they had been tricked by wicked men into putting Christ to death.

Acts 2:23-24 [23]"This man was handed over to you by God's set purpose and foreknowledge; and **you**, with the help of wicked men, **put him to death** by nailing him to the cross. [24]But God raised him from the dead, freeing him from the agony of death, because it was impossible for death to keep its hold on him."

Next we see Peter building on the knowledge of his audience. The Israelites would have known about King David and the prophecies involving him, in particular the prophecy in 2 Samuel 7:11-16 that says a king will rise up from the House of David and reign forever. In Acts 2:25-36 Peter is also aided in his sermon by his location. Apparently he was preaching near the grave of David. He uses the fact that David is dead, but Christ has risen from the dead and is now with God. He is letting them know that the King they had been waiting for, the King they had been studying about their entire life, is the King they had just put to death.

> Acts 2:36 Therefore let all Israel be assured of this: God has made this Jesus, **whom you crucified**, both Lord and Christ."

Did you know that Christ is not the last name of Jesus? Christ means messiah, anointed one, or literally king. Christ is a title, not a last name. Jesus is our King. The impact of killing a king was tremendous. This realization must have struck his audience like a lightning bolt. We see that they were "cut to the heart" and had to know what to do to fix the problem. They could not wait; they interrupted Peter and asked the fundamental question we should all ask.

> Acts 2:37 [37]When the people heard this, they were cut to the heart and said to Peter and the other apostles, **"Brothers, what shall we do?"**

I have had the opportunity to help sell products and services for my work. One of the best pieces of advice my sales friends tell me is this, "Stop selling when you get the order." Once a customer gives you an order, stop selling. In this case, Peter had his audience right where he wanted them. The question the crowd asked Peter is the fundamental question we should all be asking. Once his audience asked him, he did not continue telling them how wrong they were. He stopped his sermon and answered their question.

> Acts 2:38-39 [38]Peter replied, **"Repent and be baptized**, every one of you, in the name of Jesus Christ for the forgiveness of your sins. And you will receive the gift of the Holy Spirit. [39]The promise is for you and your children and for all who are far off—for all whom the Lord our God will call."

Repent means to say you are sorry and to change your ways. Baptize comes from the Greek word *baptidzo* and literally means to dip, plunge, submerge, or immerse. Peter had sculpted a beautiful sermon. The words repent and baptize were common and well-understood words to his audience. In Acts 2:40-41 we see that they did not argue over the meanings; they just obeyed. The first sermon was nothing less than grand. What else should we expect for the grand opening of Christ's church? Peter, the apostle who betrayed Jesus a few weeks before, was now standing in front of what could have been a mob and was preaching the first official sermon. The kingdom is now open, and already 3,000 people have walked through the doors.

Kingdom in Place

Prior to Peter's first sermon, we are told the kingdom of God is in the future. All references talk about the kingdom being near. However, after this occasion, we see people being added to the kingdom. This implies that the kingdom is now in place. Take for example the following passage from Colossians.

> Colossians 1:13 For he has rescued us from the dominion of darkness and **brought us into the kingdom** of the Son he loves . . . .

The phrase "brought into the kingdom" implies that the kingdom was in place. So far we have seen that the foundation of Christ's church sits firmly on the predictions of the prophets, the words of Jesus Christ, and the teachings of the apostles.

Acts 2:42 They devoted themselves to the **apostles' teaching** and to the fellowship, to the breaking of bread and to prayer.

Later in the New Testament Peter explains how the Kingdom is being built into a spiritual house.

> 1 Peter 2: 4-5 [4]As you come to him, the **living Stone**—rejected by men but chosen by God and precious to him— [5]you also, like living stones, are being built into a **spiritual house** to be a holy priesthood, offering spiritual **sacrifices acceptable to God** through Jesus Christ.

The living stone is Christ Himself. He set the foundation and now we are being used as spiritual bricks to build and strengthen the walls of the kingdom of heaven. This spiritual house is for the purpose of offering acceptable sacrifices to our God. If we are the spiritual bricks in the kingdom of heaven, how strong are you making the wall?

Doppler Effect

When we look at the Bible from the Old Testament to the New Testament, we can begin to appreciate the structure that Christ built for us. This did not just happen, it was planned. The best way I can think of to explain the Biblical writings concerning Christ's church is with an engineering term related to sound, the Doppler Effect. The best way to explain this is with a racetrack. Imagine you are at an Indy car race. You can see the cars coming way down the track, but you can hardly hear them. However, as they get closer, the sound starts to build. Then the sound hits a maximum pitch just as the cars pass you. As they continue past you, the sound drops back off. When we look at what Christ built, the prophet's talk about the church hundreds of years before it was opened. The Israelites could not make out exactly what was coming. Then Christ comes and He spends three years preparing the apostles and the people for the church He was about to establish. The sound or anticipation was at an all time high as the grand opening of the church happened. Then after the grand opening, we see the apostles helping people learn what it means to be part of the kingdom of God. In picture form, this looks like the following.

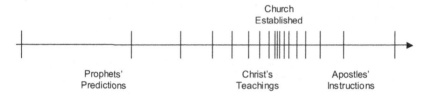

Figure 7: Biblical Doppler Effect

Foundation Is Set

As we saw in Ephesians, this massive structure of Christ's church requires a foundation that will not crack.

> Ephesians 2:19-21 [19]Consequently, you are no longer foreigners and aliens, but fellow citizens with God's people and members of God's household, [20]built on **the foundation of the apostles and prophets, with Christ Jesus himself as the chief cornerstone**. [21]In him the whole building is joined together and rises to become a holy temple in the Lord.

The foundation of Christ's church is iron clad and unchanging. The foundation is not growing and there are no additions being made. There are no new prophets, there is no other Christ, and there are no new apostles. **The Church that Christ Built** can be clearly found in the Scriptures, but we have to look. If we do not understand the significance of this structure, our lack of understanding does not make the structure less important. If we do not understand or appreciate what Christ did for us, then we need to study to find out why entering the kingdom is such a big deal to Christ.

Miraculous Spiritual Gifts

Exclamation Point

Which phrase is stronger, "Come here" or "Come here!"? Typically the phrase with the exclamation point is read with greater emphasis. That is why we have exclamation points. In the written language, emphasis is added to the phrase or word when one is added. In a similar fashion, God adds emphasis to His word with miraculous spiritual gifts.

Miraculous spiritual gifts are different than spiritual gifts. For example, if my daughter is sick and I pray that she gets better and she does, I would classify that as God answering a prayer. An answered prayer is a form of a spiritual gift. A miraculous spiritual gift on the other hand has to do with events that go beyond the laws of nature. For example, if I pick up my pencil and let go of it, but the pencil stays in the air, that would be a miracle.

All through the Bible we read of miracles. In the New Testament, the concept of miraculous spiritual gifts is used to define things like instant healing, foreknowledge, and speaking in tongues. Some of the more readily known examples of instant healings have to do with raising Lazarus from the dead (John 11), restoring sight to the blind (Matthew 20), making lame men walk (Mark 2), and stopping the bleeding woman by a simple touch of Christ's garment (Matthew 9). In Matthew we see how people brought their sick to Christ to be healed.

> Matthew 15:30-31 [30]Great crowds came to him, bringing the lame, the blind, the crippled, the mute and many others, and laid them at his feet; and he healed them. [31]The **people were amazed** when they saw the mute speaking, the crippled made well, the lame walking and the blind seeing. And they praised the God of Israel.

We even see in this passage that people were amazed by what Christ was doing for their sick. Amazed and exclamation point go together. Christ used miracles to show people that He was the real thing. He was the son of God. Apostles also had the gift of performing miracles. Scriptures showing this are:
- 1 Corinthians 12:12 The things that mark an apostle—signs, wonders and miracles—were done among you with great perseverance.
- Acts 5:12 The apostles performed many miraculous signs and wonders among the people.
- Acts 2:43 Everyone was filled with awe, and many wonders and miraculous signs were done by the apostles.

We also see as the structure of **the Church that Christ built** was forming, many members of the early church also had the ability to perform miraculous spiritual gifts.

> 1 Corinthians 12:27-28 [27]Now you are the body of Christ, and each one of you is a part of it. [28]And in the church God has appointed first of all apostles, second prophets, third teachers, then **workers of miracles**, also

those having **gifts of healing**, those able to help others, those with gifts of administration, and those **speaking in different kinds of tongues**.

The fact that early Christians, the apostles and Christ did many miracles is not a question that needs to be debated. Scripture is very clear that these groups of people did have the ability to perform miraculous spiritual gifts. However, the question that does come up today is what was the purpose of these gifts and are these gifts still being practiced today? In order to answer these questions, we must dig into Scripture.

Purposes

As we evaluate the different miraculous spiritual gifts, we will see that there are three categories for the use of these gifts. They are: Inspiration, Confirmation, Impartation.

Inspiration

One of the reasons for miraculous spiritual gifts was to inspire men to great works.

- John 14:26 But the Counselor, the Holy Spirit, whom the Father will send in my name, will teach you all things and will remind you of everything I have said to you.
- Acts 1:8 But you will receive power when the Holy Spirit comes on you; and you will be my witnesses in Jerusalem, and in all Judea and Samaria, and to the ends of the earth."

These two examples show how the power given to the apostles was going to give them the strength and ability to preach the good news of Christ. At this time, the written word was still being written. If the Holy Spirit had not directed the apostles, the potential for confusion would have been great. Christ let the apostles know He was going to take care of them. This miraculous spiritual gift had to not only comfort them but also be a constant reminder of their friend and Savior Christ.

Confirmation

Confirmation has to do with validating something's reality. God used miraculous spiritual gifts to prove that His word was real. The following scriptures show us that these gifts were used to confirm the truth of God's word.

- Mark 16:20 Then the disciples went out and preached everywhere, and the Lord worked with them and confirmed his word by the signs that accompanied it.
- John 14:11 Believe me when I say that I am in the Father and the Father is in me; or at least believe on the evidence of the miracles themselves.

- Hebrews 2:3-4 How shall we escape if we ignore such a great salvation? This salvation, which was first announced by the Lord, was confirmed to us by those who heard him. 4God also testified to it by signs, wonders and various miracles, and gifts of the Holy Spirit distributed according to his will.
- Acts 14:3 So Paul and Barnabas spent considerable time there, speaking boldly for the Lord, who confirmed the message of his grace by enabling them to do miraculous signs and wonders.

In all of these verses, miraculous spiritual gifts were used to confirm or prove that Christ's words were really from God. The miracles added emphasis to what was being said and taught. After all, the early church was just coming out of years of dedication to the old law. Getting their attention was going to take more than some good sermons. Getting their attention required miraculous spiritual gifts.

Impartation
Miraculous spiritual gifts were not handed out to everyone or by just anyone. The Holy Spirit gave these gifts to the apostles and to a select few Gentiles when they were added to the kingdom (Acts 10:44-48). After these examples of miraculous spiritual gifts were handed out by the Holy Spirit, we only read of the apostles passing these gifts on to people of their choosing.
- Acts 6:6 They presented these men to the apostles, who prayed and laid their hands on them.
- Acts 8:17-18 Then Peter and John placed their hands on them, and they received the Holy Spirit.
- Acts 19:6 When Paul placed his hands on them, the Holy Spirit came on them
- 2 Timothy 1:6 the gift of God, which is in you through the laying on of my hands.

These passages show that the apostles had the ability to pass on miraculous spiritual gifts by the laying on of their hands only. We see that only the apostles had this ability in the story of Simon and the Sorcerer found in Acts 8:9-24.

Acts 8:18 When Simon saw that the Spirit was **given at the laying on of the apostles' hands,** he offered them money [19]and said, "Give me also this ability so that everyone on whom I lay my hands may receive the Holy Spirit."

Simon wanted to purchase the gift from the apostles. If others could have passed on these gifts, why didn't Simon go to one of those who had the gift already? Instead, he went directly to the apostles in hopes of being able to get this gift from them. His plan backfired, but this passage shows that miraculous spiritual gifts were given based on the needs of the apostles.

Frequency of Use in the Early Church

The need for miraculous spiritual gifts was significant in the New Testament. The early Christians who were first added to the kingdom needed to see these gifts practiced often. They would have needed to see them to be reminded of the greatness of Christ as well as the significance of His message. In fact, the prevalence of these gifts was so strong that the apostles even had to provide instructions in 1 Corinthians 14:26-33 for when and how these gifts should be used. This passage shows that there was a need for instruction related to the use of miraculous spiritual gifts. Otherwise, there would have been no need to tell the early church how they should be used. Notice that in these instructions, the purpose of the gifts is to strengthen, instruct, and encourage Christians. Also notice that these gifts were to be used in an orderly manner.

Time-line of Recorded Uses

We see in the last passage that miraculous spiritual gifts were so common that the apostles had to provide instructions related to their use in worship. However, if we look at the approximate dates related to subsequent references to the use of miraculous spiritual gifts, we start to see an interesting pattern emerging.

- AD 38 - Acts 19:11-12 - Even handkerchiefs and aprons that had touched Paul were taken to the sick and their illnesses were cured and the evil spirits left them.
- AD 55 - 1 Corinthians 14:26 – Paul instructs the early church on how to the use miraculous spiritual gifts.
- AD 60 - James 5:14-15 - healing was still practiced.
- AD 64 - Colossians 4:14-15 - Paul referrers to Luke as the "beloved physician."
- AD 65 - 1 Timothy 5:23; 2 Timothy 4:20 - Paul recommended medicine for Timothy and left Trophimus at Miletus sick.
- AD 90 and AD 96 - 1st, 2nd, and 3rd John and Revelation were all written after the fall of Jerusalem. None of these books make reference of miracles, healings, or spiritual gifts being performed in the church.

This time-line shows that for several years after the church was established, the use of miraculous spiritual gifts was quite common. However, as we progress toward the end of the New Testament, we see much fewer references to miraculous spiritual gifts. Some say this is because they were so common there was no need to talk about them. If that were true, why is it that we see Paul giving medicine to people and in some cases leaving them sick? After all, at the height of spiritual gifts, people only needed to touch Paul's handkerchief and they were healed. Another answer for the decline of recorded instances of miraculous spiritual gifts has to do with the second purpose of these gifts, confirmation. Once something is confirmed to be true, there is no need to reconfirm the truth later. In AD 70, Hebrews 2:3 tells us "**This salvation**, which was first announced by the Lord, **was confirmed** to us by those who heard him." The truth related to Christ had been confirmed to us by the writings of Scripture by AD 70. As a result, there is no need to add emphasis to a point already made. The following plot shows how the frequency of recorded miraculous spiritual gifts drops as the truth of God is written and confirmed.

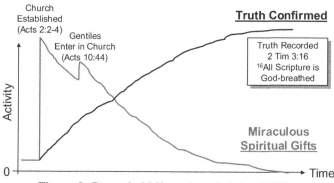

Figure 8: Recorded Miraculous Spiritual Gifts

Christ told His apostles that His church would start with a great show of power. The great show of power was the Holy Spirit coming and landing on these men. What a grand opening to the Kingdom. Once Christ went back to heaven, the apostles were left to carry on the message. The miraculous spiritual gifts gave them strength and courage in order to prove the word of God was real. However, as time marched on and more of God's word was written, the need to keep confirming the truth with miracles faded away. Today miraculous spiritual gifts are not needed since God's revelation has been fully delivered.

Closing Comments
Miraculous New Testament spiritual gifts were used to emphasize the importance of the Kingdom of heaven and to confirm the revelation of God. The grand opening of **the Church that Christ Built** was amazing. God's use of miraculous spiritual gifts was just right and when the Word was confirmed, the need for miraculous spiritual gifts was no more. We read of this in 1 Corinthians 13.

1 Corinthians 13:13 **[8]Love never fails. But where there are prophecies, they will cease; where there are tongues, they will be stilled; where there is knowledge, it will pass away.** [9]For we know in part and we prophesy in part, [10]but when perfection comes, the imperfect disappears. [11]When I was a child, I talked like a child, I thought like a child, I reasoned like a child. When I became a man, I put childish ways behind me. [12]Now

we see but a poor reflection as in a mirror; then we shall see face to face. Now I know in part; then I shall know fully, even as I am fully known. [13]And now **these three remain: faith, hope and love. But the greatest of these is love**.

This passage teaches us that even if miraculous spiritual gifts were present, they mean nothing without love. In fact, no matter what talent we may have, that talent means nothing if we don't have love for each other. In verse 13 we see that the only gifts that remain are faith, hope, and love. We also see that of these three, the greatest gift is love. All too often, people will strive after riches, talents, or even miraculous spiritual gifts. These people are in danger of missing out on the greatest gift of all, the love of Christ when He returns. If we lose focus and shift our sights away from the love of Christ and the love of each other, we run the risk of hearing Christ Himself tell us in person that He never knew us.

Matthew 7:21-23 [21]Not everyone who says to me, "Lord, Lord," will enter the kingdom of heaven, but only he who does the will of my Father who is in heaven. [22]Many will say to me on that day, "Lord, Lord, **did we not prophesy in your name, and in your name drive out demons and perform many miracles?**" [23]Then I will tell them plainly, "**I never knew you. Away from me, you evildoers!**"

I have shared these points with people in the past, but they usually respond with, "How can you not believe in modern-day miraculous spiritual gifts?" Their response defines the problem. We are to believe in Christ, not miraculous spiritual gifts.

Questions to Consider
1. How does a mountain and the Church that Christ Built relate?
2. Name several examples of miraculous spiritual gifts described in the Bible.
3. Name several examples of spiritual gifts that we have today.
4. Would the message of Christ and the apostles have been as strong without miraculous spiritual gifts?

Chapter 8: Time for Expansion

A Picture Paints a Thousand Words

Do you know what a shutterbug is? If ever there was one, it would be my dad. I think he was born with a camera in his hands. When I was a kid, he even set up a darkroom in the basement so he could take more pictures. He never seems to have a problem taking pictures of people or things. Now that he has grandchildren, he has not slowed down one bit. I am afraid my kids thought my dad was a star because every time they saw him, a flash was going off. I remember when Kim and I were going to watch my daughter march in her first Christmas parade. We had forgotten our camera, but fortunately my Dad was there to save the day with his camera. They say a picture is worth a thousand words. I can look at some of my Dad's old pictures and instantly be taken back in time. I am thankful my dad is a shutterbug and hope he keeps it up for a long time. In the last chapter we ended with Peter's first sermon. The church was now established, people were being converted, and they were devoting themselves to the apostle's teaching. The remainder of Acts chapter 2, we get to see a word picture of the early church.

The "Garden of Eden" Period

During the first few months as **the Church that Christ Built** was adding members, there were no denominations, just unity. There was no fighting, just mutual admiration. There were no hard feelings, just awe and respect for the Lord. Fortunately, the life of the early church was recorded for us to read. The closest thing to a camera back then was pen and paper.

> Acts 2:42-47 [42]They **devoted themselves** to the apostles' teaching and to the fellowship, to the breaking of bread and to prayer. [43]Everyone was **filled with awe**, and many wonders and miraculous signs were done by the apostles. [44]All **the believers were together** and had everything in common. [45]Selling their possessions and goods, they gave to anyone as he had need. [46]**Every day they continued to meet together** in the temple courts. They broke bread in their homes and ate together with glad and sincere hearts, [47]**praising God and enjoying the favor of all the people**. And the Lord added to their number daily those who were being saved.

In these few verses we get to see a wonderful time, a time to which we should all be striving to return. We see that the early Christians were: Unwavering in commitment (vs 42), Filled with awe (vs 43), Unselfish in compassion (vs 45), Enjoying each other (vs 46), United in Christ (vs 47). In order to bring the picture these verses are trying to portray into focus, we will take a closer look at each one of these areas.

Unwavering in Commitment

A young man wrote the following note to his soon-to-be wife.

> "Dear Love,
> I long to see you this weekend, the days drag on for hours when we are apart. When I close my eyes, I can feel your skin and smell your hair. I want you to know how much I love you. I would cross the tallest mountains and swim the deepest oceans just to be near you. Oh, how I long to be near you soon.
> Love, Your Prince
> P.S. I will be over Friday night if it does not rain."

I am pretty sure this story is what is called a "preacher's story," but it illustrates the fickleness of wavering devotion.

We see in Acts 2:42 the early Christians were devoted to the apostles' teachings. They could not get enough of it. The feeling going through the new Christians would almost be like us living in a time when candles were all that could be used to light up a room. In the light of a candle, we probably would have had a spotless house. Then, the electric company brings power down our lane and gives us our first light bulb. Once that new light is turned on, we now see our house in a completely different light. Sorry for the pun. However, it would be true. Things we once took for granted as being clean and in order would now look old and dingy. We would most likely do our best to get things in order now that we could more clearly. The early church was in the same predicament. They had been living under the Jewish law of the Old Testament, but now they were shown the light of the New Testament, Christ.

They could not get enough, and once they saw what they were supposed to do, they devoted themselves not only to this new teaching, but also to each other. We see in verse 42 that they also devoted themselves to fellowship. Fellowship is simply spending time with each other. Being devoted to something means that something is a top priority in one's life. The early Christians were devoted to the apostles' teaching and to fellowship. This meant that being with each other and learning about Christ was the most important aspects of their life.

I once invited a friend to church. While we were at church, many of my church friends introduced themselves and tried to start up conversations. However, my new friend was pretty reserved about all of this. Later I asked if there was a problem. He told me he felt church was a time for a personal relationship with God and should not involve talking to others. I thought to myself, "Is this what it means to be devoted to fellowship?" I found out later that my friend had been brought up in a religion that did not advocate personal relationships with members, but a personal relationship only with Jesus. I never got a second chance to bring him to church with me. How sad. His mental database had been set a long time ago with a doctrine that is foreign to the Scriptures. So foreign that when confronted with **the Church that Christ built**, he felt awkward.

If you take a blanket and lay it out flat on the floor, then grab the center of the blanket and slowly start lifting straight up, what happens? All the pieces of the blanket come together. This is not magic, but it illustrates what happens when people devote themselves to Christ. As we focus on Christ, we all naturally come together like the ends of the blanket. There is no way around it. As we start to look more and more like Christ, we start to enjoy being around each other. You cannot have a focus on Christ and not like fellowship.

Not only did the early Christians enjoy spending time together, we see at the end of verse 42 that they broke bread and prayed together. The term "broke bread" usually refers to the Lord's Supper.

> 1 Corinthians 16:16-17 ¹⁶Is not the cup of thanksgiving for which we give thanks a participation in the blood of Christ? And is not the **bread that we break** a participation in the body of Christ? ¹⁷Because there is one loaf, we, who are many, are one body, for we all partake of the one loaf.

The early Christians devoted themselves to partaking of the Lord's Supper. Why do you think the Lord's Supper was so important that they devoted themselves to it? The last verse actually helps us answer that. We see that the Lord's Supper was not for getting full on physical food but was for the purpose of remembering Christ. They had just found out they had a hand in killing the Lord. So they obviously did not know Him, but now they desperately are trying to learn and remember Him. The Lord's Supper was designed for that purpose, to remember Christ.

The early Christians also devoted themselves to prayer. Prayer is nothing more than talking to God. Christ wants to hear from us. The early Christians had ignored Him while He was with them. Now they devoted themselves to talking with Him. In this one small verse, we see the early Christians longed to learn of Christ. Since Christ was now gone, they flocked to the apostles to learn from them. They now talked with Him through prayer, remembered Him with the Lord's Supper, and strengthened each other through fellowship.

Filled with Awe

In verse 43, we see that the early Christians were filled with awe. The word awe brings up many mental pictures. One Sunday at our church service, I looked over and saw a new dad holding his 1-month-old baby. Awe came to my mind. One summer my family went to the Grand Canyon. When we stood at the rim, we were filled with a sense of awe. The word awe fits in both examples.

However, the early Christians were now devoting themselves to Christ. This devotion comes from a realization of the magnitude of Christ. The awe my family felt while looking into the Grand Canyon was nothing short of spectacular. However, the awe the early Christians felt was even bigger. They were now part of the body of Christ, they were part of a new covenant, and they were seeing the power of God at the hands of the apostles. Ephesians helps us see how the Old Testament was replaced with the New Testament. The early Christians would have come to this realization.

> Ephesians 2:14-15 [14]For he himself is our peace, who has made the two one and has destroyed the barrier, the dividing wall of hostility, [15]by abolishing in his flesh the law with its commandments and regulations. His purpose was to create in himself one new man out of the two, thus making peace;

Their understanding of what they had missed with Christ coupled with what they had been given by Christ had to make them feel unworthy. The gift of God had been given to them, but they had killed God's Son. This does not equate. This does not make sense, but it happened and the early Christians were the first to walk through the doors of **the Church that Christ built**. They were given a gift that was beyond their ability to understand or even imagine. This realization comes close to defining the awe the early Christians were feeling. The awe they felt is the same awe we should feel today, and that is a love for Christ that words cannot express.

Unselfish in Compassion

I once heard a story about a preacher tryout. When that Sunday came for the tryout, everyone at the church was excited to hear this new fellow. None of them knew who he was or expected to see him until he stood up to preach. However, when the time for the sermon came, no one stood up. Everyone looked at each other and thought that maybe the new guy was nervous and trying to capture his composure. However, after about 5 minutes of sitting in awkward silence, one of the elders finally stood up and indicated that their new guy must be a no show. About that time, a guy came running up the aisle quite winded and apologized for being late. He introduced himself as the preacher trying out. He then took a long look at the congregation. He took his time making eye contact with each family before he told them why he was late. Here is what he said, "As you know, you have a long driveway, maybe a mile long that goes up the side of this hill to get to your beautiful building. My car is a little old and it decided to give up the ghost at the foot of the hill. I patiently waited for someone to stop and help me. However, as I watched each of you drive by, I realized I would have to walk." The church fell silent. They now recognized the fellow at the foot of the hill and to their shame; no one had stopped to help him. This is supposed to be a true story. I am embarrassed for that congregation.

We can get so caught up with the mechanics of Christianity that we forget to be Christian. Being late to church or stopping to help a person who is broken down on the side of the street should not be a major decision to make. However, if we do not make an effort to be aware of our surroundings, then compassion for others takes a backseat.

The early Christians during this "Garden of Eden" time had not only compassion for each other, but unselfishness as well. Consider for a moment a young man who is about to purchase a car. He has been saving for a long time and finally has enough money. He goes to the dealer, negotiates a good price, and drives off with a new car. He is feeling pretty good about his car and his decision when bang, he is hit. Luckily, no one is hurt. The young man is a little stunned when the person who hit him runs up to see if he is OK. The young man indicates that he is fine and then gets out of his now-totaled car. The person that hit him says, "You are taking this accident pretty well." The young man replies, "Well, this car belongs to God, and if God wants to smash up a perfectly good car, then that is His prerogative." Wouldn't it be nice if we could disengage ourselves from our stuff? That is not to say we treat the things in our care badly, but rather to realize that we are stewards of God's possessions. If only we could grow to the point where we realize that God owns everything, then how would we treat a brother or sister in need?

I can't help but think we would respond in much the same way as we see the early Christians respond to the needs of others. The early Christians responded with an unselfish compassion for each other. In verse 45, we see that they sold their possessions and goods so that they could give to anyone in need. Why did the early Christians do this? There would most likely have been an abundance of people in need. At the time of the opening of the kingdom, there would have been a rush of people in Jerusalem as a result of Pentecost. Many of these Jews were becoming members of **the Church that Christ built.** Some historians estimate that over 30,000 Christians were added within the first few months.

Most likely these new Christians had not come to Jerusalem to stay; they would have gone home shortly after Pentecost. However, this Pentecost was different. Their entire worship practice had been changed and they now were getting the chance to "see" Jesus for the first time. They did not want to leave. As a result, many would have needed places to stay, food to eat, and clothes to wear. The early Christians banded together and saw to it that everyone's needs were met.

Have you ever had the opportunity to help someone before they asked for it? I have one personal example that comes quickly to mind. One winter several years ago, I noticed that one of our older men at church was wearing a light windbreaker in the dead of winter. I happened to have a leather coat on one Wednesday night when I realized that I was about the same size as this fellow. I went up to him and asked him if he would try on my coat. I told him I wanted to see if it would fit him. He did not think anything of my request and he tried the coat on. The coat did fit and it looked good on him. He was about to take the coat off when I told him to keep the coat. I did not give him the coat in hopes he would give me money, recognition, or anything. I saw a fellow who needed a coat. Mine fit him so I gave it to him, no strings attached. There is something about unselfish compassion that words cannot describe. Some people call this "practicing random acts of kindness". There are literally hundreds of ways to help others in need on a daily basis. However, for us to recognize these opportunities we have to pay attention.

I would be remiss if I did not provide the rest of the story. Several years had gone by since I had given away that coat. Then one day we were collecting donations for a give-away day at our church. We got a call from an elderly family who was moving to Florida. They had heard of our program and wanted to donate many of their things. I had a van and happened to live close to this family. So I went over and started collecting the items they wanted to donate. As we were finishing up, the elderly man looked at me and asked me what size suit jacket I wore. I told him and he smiled. He just realized that since he was moving to Florida, he would not need any of his winter suits or topcoats. He then went into his house and came back with several hundred dollars' worth of the finest winter dress clothes I had ever seen. They all fit like a glove. The gentleman was thrilled and then told me to keep them all. I offered to pay him, but he would not take a cent. To this day, I still have these items and I am still not only humbled by this man's kindness, but I am also impressed with God's generosity. Practice **unselfish** compassion and I know that one day God will reward your efforts.

United in Christ

The first few months of the early church were nothing less than awesome. The early Christians were learning from the apostles about Christ, they were seeing the power of God through the miracles performed by the apostles, and they did not think twice about helping each other. This type of atmosphere fuels positive relationships. We also see Acts 2:44-47 that early Christians spent a considerable amount of time together. Consider these phrases: The believers were together, they had everything in common, they continued to meet together every day, they ate together, and they enjoyed the favor of all the people. No wonder the early church was growing so fast. The movement would have snuffed itself out if they had spent their time debating religious doctrines and finding fault in each other. However, this Christian movement did not snuff itself out. Rather, it was exploding. During this "Garden of Eden," the Christians were united. They were united in their belief about Christ and their resolve to make Him proud. They were excited about the new knowledge of Christ and they could not help but to tell their friends about Him.

The unity of Christians is a common theme in the New Testament. There are many writings that focus on the body of Christ and how it is to function. The Bible is very clear that the body is to be united. The following three passages: 1 Corinthians 12:12, 1 Corinthians 12:24-27, and Ephesians 4:16 give us insights as to what Christ expects of His body, the church. The early church had not read these passages yet. In fact, these passages had not yet been written. The unity of the early church was a direct result of their desire and focus to learn about Jesus.

Imagine the concept of a bicycle wheel. In order for the wheel to spin true, all the spokes have to be tightened just right. Each spoke has an adjustment and each spoke is tied to the center of the wheel. Christians are the body of Christ, we are all to look toward Christ, and we are all to make adjustments to be sure Christ is the focal point of our life. When we are out of alignment with Christ's will, the wheel won't spin true. Colossians 3:12-14 shows us that we are to wrap ourselves in the love of Christ so we can be members with His body. Bond in perfect unity!

The early Christians had love for each other. They were the first Christians. They depended on each other to survive. The idea of leaving the group to find another group was a foreign concept. There were no other Christian groups. Maybe this is why they worked so well together. They did not abandon the faith when they came across something they did not understand or agree with. They worked together to find a solution. The early Christians had one significant benefit that we do not have today. Since they were the first ones to enter the Kingdom, they did not have years of bad habits to break. They all realized they knew nothing about being a Christian. However, they knew where to find the answers. The answers were with the apostles and that is why they devoted themselves to their teachings. The new Christians were like sponges soaking up the good news of Christ. There was an atmosphere of love, compassion, thanksgiving, and a hunger for knowledge about Jesus. The early Christians were not just unified - they were unified in Christ.

A Look Back

Rapid Church Growth

The love the early church had for each other and for Christ is evident in these few verses in Acts, chapter 2. Their devotion to each other's needs, coupled with their desire to be like Christ, was the fuel that ignited early church growth. The Bible tells us several times in the first few chapters of Acts that the number of believers continued to grow.

- Acts 2:41 Those who accepted his message were baptized, and about **3000 were added** to their number that day.
- Acts 2:47 And the Lord **added to their number daily**.
- Acts 4:4,14 Number of **men up to 5000,** Number of Christians **grew**.

- Acts 6:1, 7 Number of disciples **kept growing, grew rapidly.**
- Acts 9:31, 11:21, 14:21, 16:5, 16:15, 17:4, 17:12, 17:34, 19:20 A **great number** of people believed.

The writer started off with actual numbers and then changed to just say their numbers were growing. When I read these I think of the McDonald's hamburger sign. When I was a kid, it seemed like once you would order a hamburger, they would run out and change the sign. Now, they just say billions served. This is what was happening to the early church. The movement was growing so fast that keeping up with physical numbers was no longer possible. In fact, some historians estimate that the number of Christians was well over 30,000 within the first few months. Have you ever stopped to think where these people met? We see that they met in homes, but it would not be a stretch to think that they would still have met in some of the Jewish synagogues. In fact, some historians feel that entire synagogues may have been converted at once. We will see that, for a time, Jews and Christians would meet together. The Jews would refer to the Christians as the "Nazarene sect." However, it does not take long before the Jewish community wants to get rid of this "troublesome bunch."

Acts 24:5, 6 We have found this man to be a **troublemaker**, stirring up riots among the Jews all over the world. He is a ringleader of the **Nazarene sect** and even tried to desecrate the temple.

We will get into trouble like the early church soon enough, but let's first take a step backwards and study the fundamentals of the synagogue. After all, the synagogue had been the only religious center in their lives up to this point. So understanding more about where the early Christians came from can help us see where they were going.

The Synagogue

The synagogue was the center of Jewish community life. According to Eldred Echols in his book, *The Most Excellent Way*, the function of the synagogue was much more than a church. The synagogue has several functions including:
- A school, guest house, and social center.
- A center of ministries for the sick, needy, orphans, and elderly.
- A court of justice, a place to study the law.

Prior to the establishment of **the Church that Christ Built**, the Greek word used for synagogue was the same as the word we use today for church, ekklesia. We have already seen that ekklesia means an assembly or group. The terms church and synagogue were almost interchangeable until later in the New Testament when the church was firmly established. Once the church was established, the term synagogue usually referred to the place of Jewish worship, and the term church was used to define the assembly of Christian worship.

Some historians believe that by A.D. 70 when the temple was destroyed, there were 480 synagogues in Jerusalem alone. There was only one temple and it was reserved for special feasts, offering sacrifices, and ceremonies. However, there were synagogues all over the place. The mere number of synagogues present at the time of the apostles helps to explain why Jesus and the apostles made a habit of going there first when preaching of Jesus.

- Mathew 4:23 Jesus went throughout Galilee, **teaching in their synagogues**, preaching the good news of the kingdom, and healing every disease and sickness among the people.
- Matthew 12:9 Going on from that place, he (Jesus) **went into their synagogue**,
- Matthew 13:54 Coming to his (Jesus') hometown, he **began teaching the people in their synagogue**, and they were amazed. "Where did this man get this wisdom and these miraculous powers?" they asked.
- Mark 1:21 Jesus went into the **synagogue** and began to teach.
- John 18:20 "I have spoken openly to the world," Jesus replied. "I **always taught in synagogues or at the temple, where all the Jews come together**. I said nothing in secret."
- Luke 4:16, Acts 17:2 As **his custom**, Paul went into the **synagogue**,
- Acts 17:17 he (Paul) reasoned in the **synagogue** with the Jews and the God-fearing Greeks, as well as in the marketplace day by day with those who happened to be there.

The synagogue was a perfect place for Jesus and the apostles to start teaching. The audience would have been Jews who wanted to know more about Scripture and the Law. So when Jesus and the apostles would teach, they would have had a receptive audience. The apostles were a common fixture at synagogues and the temple. The Jewish leaders knew them and they knew of the movement they were trying to start. At first, the Jewish leaders considered the Christian movement as just another division in Judaism, as we read in Acts 24: 5, 6. After all, according to Mr. Echols, there were already several different Jewish groups such as the Essenes, Herodians, Pharisees, Sadducces, Libertines, Alexandrians, etc. So, to them, the Christian movement was just another group. However, as more and more people were converting to Christianity, the Jewish leaders realized this new "Nazarene sect" was something much different. We get a glimpse of how different when the Jewish Christians were talking to Paul.

Acts 21:20 Then they said to Paul: "You see, brother, how many thousands of Jews have believed, and all of them are zealous for the law. [21]They have been informed that you teach all the Jews who live among the Gentiles to

turn away from Moses, telling **them not to circumcise their children or live according to our customs.**"

Paul was teaching that the old customs and laws were no longer required. This message was a tremendous change to the Jews. This religious change was not only about doctrine, it was about a way of life. Many of the Jews could not accept Jesus and even tried to kill Paul for his teachings (Acts 21:27-32).

The synagogue and the laws of the Old Testament were such a part of Jewish life that leaving that lifestyle would have been extremely difficult. I think we sometimes give the Jews a hard time for not accepting the message of Christ. However, change rarely comes easy. Imagine that you are from a long line of farmers. The family assumes that each generation will take over the family business. So far, all of your ancestors have devoted themselves to the family business and now it is your turn. However, you don't like to farm and you want to try something different. I would hope that your family would encourage you to try your new ideas. However, your family may see your new idea as a slap in the face and do whatever they can to change your mind. I think making a dramatic change like this could be quite difficult.

Conversion Road Blocks

I got a much better appreciation of what it means to put on the name of Christ when I was in India. Often when a young person converts to Christ, it means becoming homeless. In India the family unit is quite strong and it is not uncommon for extended families to live together, pool their money together, eat together, and take care of each other. So when one of the members decides to go against the family religion, the family just tells the person not to come back. That family member is then faced with some big questions: Where will I go? What will I eat? Who will take care of me? Do I stay with a known commodity or take this leap of faith? How devoted do you have to be to Christ to walk away from this earthly security blanket? The stories my Christian brothers told me in India were amazing. They had developed such a strong faith in Christ that they knew He would take care of them, no matter what. Their strong faith and what they had given up to wear the name Christ humbled me. Of course, in their mind they had not given up anything but had gained eternal life. I am thankful I did not have to make those types of decisions when I became a Christian. However, when you compare their faith in Christ to mine, I have some growing to do.

The Jews of the New Testament had to make similar decisions to put on the name of Christ. The center of the community and the place of learning was the synagogue. Not being allowed to participate in the synagogue meant you were on the bad list and you were trouble. The following few passages show us a picture similar to what I saw in India.

- John 12:42 Yet at the same time many even among the leaders believed in him. But because of the Pharisees they **would not confess their faith for fear they would be put out of the synagogue;**
- John 16:2 They will **put you out of the synagogue**; in fact, a time is coming when anyone who kills you will think he is offering a service to God.
- Acts 9:1 Meanwhile, Saul was still breathing out murderous threats against the Lord's disciples. He went to the high priest and asked him for letters to the synagogues in Damascus, so that if he found any there who belonged to **the Way**, whether men or women, he might **take them as prisoners** to Jerusalem.

These passages show us that the Jews knew that putting on the name of the Christ would likely cause divisions in their family, friends, and community. This is why I find the "Garden of Eden" period of **the Church that Christ built** so compelling. The very first Christians knew that putting on Christ would cause them earthly problems. However, once Peter explained to them what they had done to Christ, they changed their hearts and longed to follow Him and learn of His ways. Is it any wonder, then, that they would have come together? Where else would they go? Is it any wonder they would take care of each other? Who else would have taken care of them? Is it any wonder that they devoted themselves to the apostles' teachings? No one else had the message of Christ. The early Christians we read of in Acts 2:42-47 had a love and devotion for each other that was unprecedented. They realized they were part of a movement that was bigger than anything that had ever been. I wish we could say that the "Garden of Eden" period of the church continued without incident. However, Satan could not let that happen. Jews were converting to Christ in huge numbers and things were going very well. These are things Satan can't stand, and as we will soon see, trouble was just around the corner.

Growing Pains

The early church was growing rapidly, and with that growth came opportunities for problems. The first sign of trouble came after the second recorded sermon. The first sermon was by Peter and the other apostles on the day of Pentecost. This resulted in 3,000 Christians being added to the Kingdom. This change was not enough to get the Jewish leaders concerned. However, at the second sermon in Acts, chapter 4, when thousands were added to the Kingdom, the Jewish leaders took notice.

Troubles From Outside

The story starts in Acts chapter 3, when Peter and John went into the temple to pray. As they were going in, a man who had been lame since birth asked them for money. Peter told him he had no money but would give him what he had.

That gift of Peter was to make the man walk. The lame man must have made quite a commotion because a crowd formed.

Acts 3:11 All the people were astonished and came running to them in the place called Solomon's Colonnade. [12]When Peter saw this, he said to them: "Men of Israel, why does this surprise you?"

Now that Peter had a crowd, he seized the opportunity and started his second sermon. In acts 4:1-4 we read that they went on to tell them about Christ and what they had done to him. His sermon was effective because thousands were added to the kingdom. However, it also got the Sanhedrin involved. The Sanhedrin was the governing body concerning religious law. This is why the temple priests and temple captains took Peter and John to see them. The message of Peter and John was different from the old law and if their message was true, the temple workers would be out of a job. So they did what they would have always done when someone was doing something contrary to what their teachings suggested, they went to the Sanhedrin. When Peter and John were taken to the rulers, elders, and teachers of the law, they were asked, "By what power or by what name did you heal this lame man?" Peter was not one to miss an opportunity to talk about Jesus, so he started once again.

Acts 4: 8-12 [8]Then Peter, filled with the Holy Spirit, said to them: "Rulers and elders of the people! [9]If we are being called to account today for an act of kindness shown to a cripple and are asked how he was healed, [10]then know this, you and all the people of Israel: It is by the name of Jesus Christ of Nazareth, whom you crucified but whom God raised from the dead, that this man stands before you healed. [11]He is 'the stone you builders rejected, which has become the capstone.' [12]Salvation is found in no one else, for there is no other name under heaven given to men by which we must be saved."

What a gutsy answer by Peter. His strong response was evidence to the Sanhedrin that Peter and John were not going away. In fact, his response caused the Sanhedrin to need some time to talk. So they asked them to leave, and they talked among themselves.

Acts 4: 16-17 "Everybody living in Jerusalem knows they have done an outstanding miracle, and we cannot deny it. [17]But to **stop this thing from spreading** any further among the people, we must warn these men to speak no longer to anyone in this name."

Notice in this last verse that even the wise men of the law realized what Peter and John had done. However, they would not accept Christ. They had to figure out a way to "stop this thing from spreading." That "thing" they were talking about was Christianity. The Sanhedrin even tried to bully Peter and John into keeping quiet (Acts 4:18-21). However, their threats fell on deaf ears. Eventually, they gave up and let the apostles go.

Trouble From Inside

Once Peter and John left the Sanhedrin, they went back to those who had believed and explained what had happened. Instead of the Sanhedrin's plan, weakening the movement, the opposite happened and the group was strengthened. Well, Satan was not about to give up, so he started a problem from the inside. The first recorded trouble within the movement appears in Acts chapter 5. The trouble is related to money. We see in the following passage that the new Christians were taking care of each other by bringing money to the apostles so that it could be distributed.

> Acts 4:32-33 [32]All the believers were one in heart and mind. No one claimed that any of his possessions was his own, but they shared everything they had. [33]With great power the apostles continued to testify to the resurrection of the Lord Jesus, and much grace was upon them all. [34]There were no needy persons among them. For from time to time those who owned lands or houses sold them, brought the money from the sales [35]and put it at the apostles' feet, and it was distributed to anyone as he had need.

The problem that shows up next has to do with pride. Apparently Ananias and his wife, Sapphira, had a problem with pride. They wanted to get in on the giving, but they wanted the apostles to think they had given all the money they had gotten from the sale of some property. The problem was that Ananias and Sapphira knew they had kept back some of the money for themselves.

> Acts 5:1-2 [1]Now a man named Ananias, together with his wife Sapphira, also sold a piece of property. [2]With his wife's full knowledge he kept back part of the money for himself, but brought the rest and put it at the apostles' feet.

This was a bad idea. Peter saw directly through the scam, and their deception ultimately cost them their lives. Satan's attempt failed to break up the church. In fact, when the Christians saw what had happened, the movement became even stronger (Acts 5:11-14).

Jealous Jewish Leaders

The number of Christians grew, along with respect for the apostles. This combination was too much for the Sanhedrin to take. In fact, we read in the next passage that the Jewish leaders were actually jealous of the apostles. So once again they put them in jail.

Acts 4:17 Then the high priest and all his associates, who were members of the party of the Sadducees, were filled with jealousy. [18]They arrested the apostles and put them in the public jail.

This time, however, we read in Acts 4:19 that the angel of the Lord steps in and releases them from jail. Not only were they miraculously released, they were told to go back to the temple and keep on preaching. I think the Lord was having some fun with the Jewish leaders. They thought they had the apostles under lock and key. However, when they went to get them, they were gone (Acts 4:21-24). This was high drama. The Jewish leaders thought they had stopped the apostles, but they were not in jail where they had left them. I can almost see them scratching their heads. Then someone finds out that the apostles are back in the temple preaching.

Acts 4:25-26 [25]Then someone came and said, "Look! The men you put in jail are standing in the temple courts teaching the people." [26]At that, the captain went with his officers and brought the apostles. They did not use force, because they feared that the people would stone them.

The apostles are preaching. This had to be troubling for the Jewish leaders. In fact we read in Acts 4:27-33 that the apostles were taken back to the Sanhedrin. The Sanhedrin was not used to telling someone the same thing twice. Verse 28 shows that the Sanhedrin could not believe they were back doing the very thing they had told them not to do. Again, Peter does not back down. I can't help but think the words of Jesus were echoing in Peter's ears. We see in an early lesson to the apostles that Jesus had warned them of this exact situation.

John 16:1-4 [1]"All this I have told you so that you will not go astray. [2]They will put you out of the synagogue; in fact, a time is coming when anyone who kills you will think he is offering a service to God. [3]They will do such things because they have not known the Father or me. [4]I have told you this, so that when the time comes you will remember that I warned you. I did not tell you this at first because I was with you."

The time was now and Peter was not forgetting his Lord. In fact, he tells the Sanhedrin that he follows God, not man. This was the straw that broke the camel's back. The Sanhedrin was now furious and wanted to kill them. Then came a voice of reason. This voice belonged to Gamaliel. He stood up and asked to address the council. The scripture tells the story in a way that needs little explanation.

Acts 4: 34-39 [34]But a Pharisee named Gamaliel, a teacher of the law, who was honored by all the people, stood up in the Sanhedrin and ordered that the men be put outside for a little while. [35]Then he addressed them: "Men of Israel, consider carefully what you intend to do to these men. [36]Some time ago Theudas appeared, claiming to be somebody, and about four hundred men rallied to him. He was killed, all his followers were dispersed, and it all came to nothing. [37]After him, Judas the Galilean appeared in the days of the census and led a band of people in revolt. He too was killed, and all his followers were scattered. [38]Therefore, in the present case I advise you: **Leave these men alone!** Let them go! For if their purpose or activity is of human origin, it will fail. [39]But if it is from God, you will not be able to stop these men; you will only find yourselves fighting against God."

I wonder if Gamaliel ever accepted the truth. After all, here we are, still talking about Christ over 2,000 years later. Scripture does not tell us, but his wise counsel cooled down the hot heads of the Sanhedrin. So instead of killing the apostles, they just beat them (Acts 4:40). Once again, the order of the Sanhedrin was lost to the apostles. They left rejoicing (Acts 4:41-42) that they had been beaten for the cause of Christ, and they kept on preaching and the number of Christians continued to grow.

Apostles Recruit Help

The church that Christ built was taking off. People were being added to their number daily. However, with this growth the number of problems rose. The apostles' efforts to teach about Christ started being choked out with doctrinal problems from within. The problem came to a head in Acts 6:1 when a group started to object about how their widows were being treated. This problem had been escalated to the attention of the apostles. The apostles, however, did not think they should be the ones solving these types of disputes. We see in the following passage a pretty strong, if not frustrated, response.

Acts 6:2 So the Twelve gathered all the disciples together and said, "It would not be right for us to neglect the ministry of the word of God in order to wait on tables."

The phrase, "wait on tables" tells us how the apostles felt about things that kept them from teaching about Jesus. However, the apostles realized that these types of problems would come up and that they would need help in order to deal with them. So they asked the congregation to nominate seven men to do this work.

Acts 6:3-4 [3]"Brothers, choose seven men from among you who are known to be full of the Spirit and wisdom. We will turn this responsibility over to them [4]and will give our attention to prayer and the ministry of the word."

I am reminded of the story in Exodus 18:13-16. We see the father-in-law of Moses, Jethro, had come over for a visit. He was able to see right away that

Moses was trying to solve all the problems himself. Jethro told him this was not good and that he should find capable men and set up a court system. Moses listened to his wise counsel. In so doing, Moses could focus on the more difficult cases, and still address all the needs of the Israelites.

The apostles had this story on their mind when they asked the congregation to nominate seven men to help them. The names of the seven have been recorded for us: Stephen, Philip, Procorus, Nicanor, Timon, Parmenas, and Nicolas. These men were not given an official title, or at least a title that was recorded. However, their job description was clear. They were to:
- Have a good reputation.
- Be full of the Spirit.
- Be full of wisdom.
- Responsible to "wait tables".

Their work not only enabled the apostles to teach the good news of Christ, but allowed for the solving of religious problems that would crop up from time to time. Having these men in place allowed the work to continue and grow even faster (Acts 6:7). The apostles made a very wise decision, for with it we start to see the structure of Christ's church taking place. This structure was timely and nothing short of divine. Recall that Jesus is the head of the church. He is in control and not about to let His church get snuffed out. He knew around the corner big changes were going to test His church.

Scattered

The church was gaining momentum in Jerusalem. In Acts 6:7 even temple priests were being converted. Now that high-ranking officials of the Jewish religion were starting to follow the Way, the Sanhedrin was really getting upset. In Acts, chapters 6 and 7 we see just how upset they were from the story of the stoning of Stephen.

Stoning of Stephen

Stephen was one of the seven men chosen to help with matters of the church. His ability to present the gospel was quite compelling, so compelling that the Jewish leaders could not keep up with him during their debates. I find it odd that the Jewish people Stephen was talking to would not concede that they might be wrong. Rather than evaluate their mental database to see if what he was saying might be true, they rejected his message and tried to have him put in jail (Acts 6:11-14). Here we have leaders of the Jewish community encouraging people to say negative things about Stephen. Apparently the bad things that were said were enough to get him brought before the Sanhedrin. However, being in front of the Sanhedrin, wrongly accused, did not intimidate Stephen. In fact, he was not only confident and ready to tell them his story, his faced had the appearance of an angel (Acts 6:15).

I would imagine those on the council would have been familiar with the message Stephen was about to present. I am sure many, if not all, had heard the message from the apostles and had been embarrassed. Now they had Stephen in front of them. The council must have realized they were losing ground. I wonder if Gamaliel was among the court this time? Based on the outcome of this story, I doubt it. The Sanhedrin asks Stephen if the charges were true. Now was Stephen's chance. He actually never even answers that question. Instead, he starts with a history lesson. Recall that the Sanhedrin were the "keepers of the law." They would have known the Old Testament inside and out. Stephen understood this and starts with Old Testament facts related to Jacob, Joseph, and Moses. These facts were nothing new. However, Stephen is using them to build up to the coming of Christ. In fact, nothing Stephen would have said up to this point would have caused a problem. He brings his message home in verse 51.

Acts 6:51-53 [51]"You stiff-necked people, with uncircumcised hearts and ears! You are just like your fathers: You always resist the Holy Spirit! [52]Was there ever a prophet your fathers did not persecute? They even killed those who predicted the coming of the Righteous One. And now you have betrayed and murdered him— [53]you who have received the law that was put into effect through angels but have not obeyed it."

Stephen has used the Old Testament to show that Christ was the one they should have recognized. They not only missed Him, they killed Him. In verse 53, we see the disappointment of Stephen in the council. The Sanhedrin felt they were the protectors of the law, but they had not obeyed it. They should have recognized Jesus, but they did not. They should have known better, but their hearts, their organizational status, and their lifestyle had not allowed them to see what the Scriptures were saying. These statements got them upset, but his next comment pushed them over the edge.

Acts 6:54-56 [54]When they heard this, they were furious and gnashed their teeth at him. [55]But Stephen, full of the Holy Spirit, looked up to heaven and saw the glory of God, and Jesus standing at the right hand of God. [56]"Look," he said, "I see heaven open and the Son of Man standing at the right hand of God."

Have you ever been to a sporting event where something exciting happens? What usually happens to the crowd? Typically, everyone stands up. The excitement is just too much to sit down while the play unfolds. I know when I watch my son play baseball, I can't sit still when he is up to bat. I am rooting for him and hoping he takes the ball out of the park. I can't help but think Jesus was feeling the same excitement toward Stephen. The excitement was building and Jesus just could not sit and watch this unfold. He stood up, almost like He was saying, "Look Father, I told you they could do it!" Stephen was about to hit one out of the park, and he got the chance to see Jesus pulling for him.

This statement of Stephen was the end of the court session. The Sanhedrin would not listen to anything else. The words of Stephen had to be like salt in a wound. They would not allow the thought of them being wrong to enter their minds. They were the governing body of the Law, not this guy. If they agreed to his words, that would be an admission of failure on their part. They had to get rid of him. So they rushed at him, dragged him out of town, and stoned him.

> Acts 6:57-58 [57]At this they covered their ears and, yelling at the top of their voices, they all rushed at him, [58]dragged him out of the city and began to stone him. Meanwhile, the witnesses laid their clothes at the feet of a young man named Saul.

Stephen had pushed their buttons, and now the Sanhedrin needed to remove this troublesome sect from among them. They enlisted Saul to go from door to door to find these Christians and put them in prison. This is the same Saul who took care of the coats for the people who were stoning Stephen. But, the story does not end here. It is just getting started.

> Acts 8:1-3 On that day a great persecution broke out against the church at Jerusalem, and all except the apostles were **scattered** throughout Judea and Samaria. [2]Godly men buried Stephen and mourned deeply for him. [3]But **Saul began to destroy the church**. Going from house to house, he dragged off men and women and put them in prison.

The Rest of the Story

The Sanhedrin thought they had crushed **the Church that Christ Built.** However, they could not have been further from the truth. We see in Acts 8:4 that the people who scattered out of Jerusalem did not go home and stay quiet. They preached wherever they went. The attempt by the Sanhedrin to kill the movement actually fueled the growth of the movement. The rest of the book of Acts tells us how **the Church that Christ Built** continued to grow. We see in Acts, chapter 9, that even Saul, their recruit to persecute the church, was converted. We then see in Acts, chapter 10, that the doors of the kingdom were opened to the Gentiles, and we see in Acts, chapter 11, that churches were being formed. There are many passages in Acts that tell us **the Church that Christ Built** just kept growing and getting stronger. Those passages include Acts 9:31, 11:21, 14:21, 16:5, 16:15, 17:4, 17:12, 17:34, 19:20.

No, the Sanhedrin had not stopped the church; their actions backfired and caused a growth explosion.

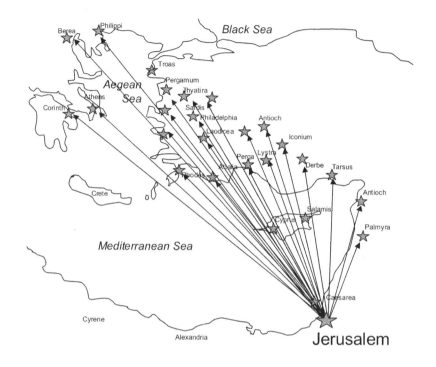

Figure 9: Scattering of the Early Church

Recall that Jerusalem was the home of the temple. The Passover was one of the required feasts, but this Passover after Christ's resurrection was different. Many on that day had become part of **the Church that Christ Built**. When the persecutions in Jerusalem became too much for them, they left and went back to their homes in many parts of the world, taking their newfound knowledge with them.

Closing Comments

I recognize the hand of God in the formation of His church. He opened the doors of His kingdom at a time and place where Jews would have been flocking to Jerusalem. The church was given time to grow and learn of Christ under the direct instruction of the apostles. It develops an infrastructure, and when the time was right, Jesus had His church spread out.

The growth of the early church was not by chance, it is a brilliant display of consistent planning and timing. After all, Christ is the head of His church, and He is still in control today.

Questions to Consider

1. Does our Church create an atmosphere where we want to do all of these things?
   - ❑ Learn of Christ
   - ❑ Partake of the Lord's Supper
   - ❑ Devote time to prayer
   - ❑ Enjoy one another's company
2. Has over 2,000 years dulled our sense of awe?
3. Does our assembly help us realize the magnitude of Christ's gift?
4. Do we feel a sense of awe when we come together for worship?
5. What are ways to pay attention to the needs of others?
6. What "random act of kindness" can you do this week?
7. How does the congregation with which you worship demonstrate love, compassion, and thanksgiving for each other?
8. Is Christ less in control of His church today that in the first century?
9. In John 9:18-23, why did the parents not answer the question concerning their son?

Chapter 9: The Lord's Army
Follow the Leader

Soldier

Jake gave me a book to read. This was a special book because it was written about his battalion when he was in World War II. I am not sure why he wanted me to read it, but he thought I would like his book. Jake was right. His battalion was part of a group of soldiers that liberated Italy. He was very proud of this book, his Purple Heart, and what his battalion had helped to do. The book was a written history talking about the lives of soldiers, their training, their fears, concerns, and their orders. Jake told me that his group would often get orders to take over this ridge, that bridge, or some house. As a soldier, he complied with all the orders, even those orders that did not make sense to him. Jake told me that it was not until he had a chance to read the entire history related to this march and the eventual victory that he understood why all of the orders from his commanding officers were given. Following orders is nothing new, especially to a soldier. Their job is to carry out orders, not debate them. Can you imagine what would happen if the soldiers in an entire squadron decided to do whatever they wanted? I can guess that squadron would fail.

Qualifications

What types of organization comes to mind when you hear the terms: Bishop, Elder, Deacon, Minister, Teacher, Reverend, or Pastor? Many recognize these as belonging to a religious organization. Next consider what determines or defines the qualifications associated with these job functions and responsibilities? What would result if the leadership names were the same for all religions, but the qualifications were completely different or even absent? How efficient can **the Church that Christ Built** be if we can't identify our leaders or their responsibilities correctly? The problem with unqualified leaders is organizational disaster. Satan would like to see **the Church that Christ Built** fail? If he can break down the organization of Christ's church, then we cannot be unified in Christ. We can't let that happen!

Early Church Organization

In the last chapter, the church continued to grow after it had been scattered from Jerusalem over the countryside. That scattering is not the last we hear of the early church. The remainder of the book of Acts tells us much about how the church developed. The interesting thing to note is that it must have known what a leader was because in many references to churches in specific areas we see that titles are used.

- Acts 11:29-30 The **disciples**, each according to his ability, decided to provide help for the **brothers** living in Judea.
- Acts 13:1 In the church at Antioch there were **prophets** and **teachers**.

- Acts 14:23 Paul and Barnabas appointed **elders** in each church.
- Acts 15:2 So Paul and Barnabas were appointed . . . to go up to Jerusalem to see the **apostles** and **elders** about this question.
- Acts 15:12 The whole **assembly** became silent as they listened.
- Acts 15:32 Judas and Silas, who themselves were **prophets**, said much to encourage and strengthen the **brothers**.
- Philemon 1:1 To all the saints in Christ Jesus at Philippi, together with the **overseers** (or **Bishops**) and **deacons**.

If we look at the bold words in these versus, we see that there must have been some type of structure in the early church:

- Apostles - Acts 15:2
- Elders - Acts 11:30, 14:23, 20:17
- Disciples and Brothers - Acts 11:29, 14:21, 14:28, 15:13, 21:17
- Evangelist - Acts 11:20
- Prophets - Acts 15:32
- Teachers - Acts 13:1
- Assembly - Acts 15:12
- Overseers and Deacons - Phil 1:1

The early Christians' use of these terms implies that they knew what the terms meant. We also see that the churches in the different areas used the same terms. This is no coincidence. They must have been taught about these positions while they were still in Jerusalem. Fortunately for us, as the New Testament is being written, we are given the specifics behind the structure of Christ's church.

Structure Defined

We see the "big picture" of the church structure in Ephesians and Colossians. In particular, we see that Christ is the Head and the church is His body.

Colossians 1:18 [18]And **he is the head of the body, the church**; he is the beginning and the firstborn from among the dead, so that in everything he might have the supremacy.

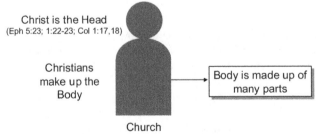

Christ is the Head
(Eph 5:23; 1:22-23; Col 1:17,18)

Christians make up the Body

Body is made up of many parts

Church

Figure 10: Structure Overview

Ephesians that the body is made up of many parts.

Ephesians 4:16 [16]From him the whole body, joined and held together by every supporting ligament, grows and builds itself up in love, as **each part** does its work.

So what are these parts? In Corinthians, we are told what the different parts are.

1 Corinthians 12: 27-28 [27]Now you are the body of Christ, and each one of you is a part of it. [28]And in the church **God has appointed** first of all **apostles**, second **prophets**, third **teachers**, then **workers of miracles**, also those having **gifts of healing**, those able to **help others**, those with **gifts of administration**, and those **speaking in different kinds of tongues**.

When we look at this verse and apply it to the structure of the church, we get a picture that looks like the following.

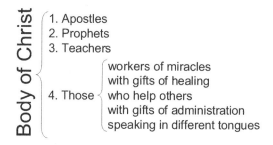

Figure 11: Structure Defined

We see that we have a living structure made up of four classes or groups of people. These groups are very important when you consider that God is the one doing the appointing. This structure has a very important job, that job is to ensure that the body of Christ has life. The structure is crucial, but a structure with no function is useless. Digging a little deeper shows us a clear functional picture.

Ephesians 4:11-13 [11]It was he (Christ) who gave some to be **apostles**, some to be **prophets**, some to be **evangelists**, and some to be **pastors** and **teachers**, [12]to **prepare** God's people for **works of service**, so that the **body of Christ may be built up** [13]until we all reach unity in the faith and in the knowledge of the Son of God and become mature, attaining to the whole measure of the **fullness of Christ**.

A diagram of this passage shows that the structure leads to function.

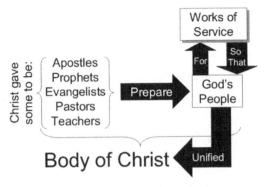

Figure 12: Functional Description

The organization's job is to prepare God's people for works of service so that they can look like Christ. What a simple plan! **The Church that Christ built** is not complicated.

Christ put an organization together that is asked to prepare us to look and act like Him. All we have to do is carry out the plan. In order for us to do that, we need to know how to recognize those individuals whom Christ has given to be Apostles, Prophets, Evangelist, Pastors, and Teachers. That task could be quite difficult for us if we had not been given the job responsibilities for each of these positions. The remainder of this section will outline what the function and job qualifications are for each of these God-given organizational roles.

Apostle

Responsibilities
The definition of apostle is simply "one sent forth." If this were the only requirement of an apostle, then there could be all kinds of apostles. Moses would even fall into this category.

Requirements
Since this definition of apostle is too broad, we need to look a little closer to determine if all those who were sent out to teach about Christ fall into the category of apostle. One of the early signs the class of people who fits the apostle definition was dramatically reduced is when Jesus picks the 12 men who were to serve as apostles (Matthew 10: 1-4). These twelve men walked with Jesus and learned from Him directly. This was an important requirement for being an apostle. We see how important this requirement was when the steps were taken to replace Judas.

Acts 2:21-22 [21]"Therefore it is necessary to choose one of the men who have **been with us the whole time** the Lord Jesus went in and out among us, [22]beginning from John's baptism to the time when Jesus was taken up from us. For one of these must become a witness with us of his resurrection."

The eleven remaining apostles found men that fit the qualification and then prayed to the Lord for direction. They did not pick a man at random.

Acts 1:23-26 [23]So they proposed two men: Joseph called Barsabbas (also known as Justus) and Matthias. [24]Then they prayed, "Lord, you know everyone's heart. **Show us** which of these two you have chosen [25]to take over this **apostolic ministry**, which Judas left to go where he belongs." [26]Then they cast lots, and the lot fell to Matthias; so he was added to the eleven apostles.

Why did the apostles need someone that had been with them? We may never know, but we do know that these apostles had a serious job in making sure the foundation of Christ's church would not crack. In Ephesians 2:20 we read why their message was so important.

[19]Consequently, you are no longer foreigners and strangers, but fellow citizens with God's people and also members of his household, [20]built on the foundation of the apostles and prophets, with Christ Jesus himself as the chief cornerstone. [21]In him the whole building is joined together and rises to become a holy temple in the Lord.

They refer to their message as the apostolic ministry. Once Christ went back to heaven, the apostles were the authority. The responsibility of ensuring that Christ was taught and that His church had a firm foundation fell only on these men. Shortly, the Lord adds another apostle to the group in the person of Paul. This is the same Paul who watched as Stephen was stoned, who had been given the task to destroy Christ's church.

Acts 9:5-6 "Who are you, Lord?" Saul asked. "I am Jesus, whom you are persecuting," he replied. [6]"Now get up and go into the city, and you will be told what you must do."

Paul in his own words talks about his appointment as an Apostle as being less than normal.

1 Corinthians 15:8 and last of all he appeared to me also, as to one abnormally born.

The 12 apostles and later Paul were the only recorded men who had the task of carrying on the apostolic ministry. Later in 2 Corinthians, we see that a further mark of an apostle was his ability to perform signs, wonders, and miracles.

> 2 Corinthians 12:12 [12]The things that **mark an apostle—signs, wonders and miracles**—were done among you with great perseverance.

The class of men called apostles is not endless and their job was critical. They played a major part in ensuring the foundation of **the Church that Christ built** was solid as a rock!

Checklist

We can summarize the requirements for an apostle with the following checklist:

- ☑ One sent forth.
- ☑ Taught by Christ.
- ☑ Tasks to teach the apostolic ministry.
- ☑ Mark of an apostle: able to perform signs, wonders, and miracles.
- ☑ Names are written in heaven.

There are no people living today who physically walked with Christ. There are no longer people with the authority of these men. This means that there are no apostles today. The church form was set, based on the teaching of only these apostles. Their teaching is part of the foundation of the church.

Prophets

Responsibility

A prophet is a teacher who relayed the message of God to His people with either current information or future insights related to God's will. In the Old Testament we regularly read of prophets. In the early church, we also regularly read of people prophesying.

> 1 Corinthians 14:6, 24-25 [6]Now, brothers, if I come to you and speak in tongues, what good will I be to you, unless I bring you some revelation or knowledge or **prophecy** or word of instruction?
>
> [24]But if an unbeliever or someone who does not understand comes in while everybody is **prophesying**, he will be convinced by all that he is a sinner and will be judged by all, [25]and the secrets of his heart will be laid bare. So he will fall down and worship God, exclaiming, "God is really among you!"

The fact that prophets were present in the early church is well documented. In fact, we see specific instructions given to prophets related to how and when they should prophesy.

Requirements

In 1 Corinthians: 29-33, 36-40, Paul provides the early church with instructions directed toward prophets. Paul provides the early church with instructions about prophets so that false prophets would not confuse the early church. In verse 38, Paul says that if a prophet ignores these instructions, then the church should ignore that prophet.

The question concerning prophets is not if prophets existed in the early church; the question is do they exist today? We see in these passages that the job of a prophet was to be a conduit for the word of God. Working in groups of two or three, they made sure what they revealed was from God and consistent. They were not to disrupt the service. Their job was to instruct and encourage, not to confuse and disrupt. Keep in mind that the Bible we have today had not been written yet. Their job was to get the word to the people. Today we have the word of God. Paul tells us it has been written and is useful for all teaching, rebuking, and correcting. He also tells us that all Scripture is God-breathed.

> 1 Timothy 3:16-17 [16]**All Scripture is God-breathed** and is useful for teaching, rebuking, correcting and training in righteousness, [17]so that the man of God may be thoroughly equipped for every good work.

Since we have God's word, are prophets needed today? Scripture tells us the answer.

1 Corinthians 13:8 [8]Love never fails. But **where there are prophecies, they will cease**; where there are tongues, they will be stilled; where there is knowledge, it will pass away. [9]For we know in part and we prophesy in part, [10]but when perfection comes, the imperfect disappears.

In this passage we are told that prophecies will cease when perfection comes. Today, we have God's written word. If we need an answer, we look it up. We don't find it outside of Scripture. As the word of God was being recorded, the need for prophets was diminished. The frequency of recorded prophecy drops quickly as the New Testament progresses. In fact, when we get to the letters of John, he does not mention them at all. Instead, John spends time talking about love.

So are there modern-day prophets? This subject is controversial and in some of today's religions we do hear of people who claim to have the gift of telling the future. However, when I hear of a modern-day prophet, I never see him or her carry out the gift as defined in 1 Corinthians 14:29. As a result, we should heed Paul's warning and ignore them.

Additionally, I have read about people who flocked to a building when they heard that a modern-day prophet was coming. The people who see this modern-day prophet tell of experiences that at first glance would seem to go beyond coincidence. However, there are two problems with these stories. First, they are not practicing the gift as the Bible defines, and second, people flock to hear about their future, not about Christ. How do you think these modern-day prophets make Jesus feel? Jesus tells us in the following passage.

Matthew 7:21-23 [21]"Not everyone who says to me, 'Lord, Lord,' will enter the kingdom of heaven, but only he who does the will of my Father who is in heaven. [22]Many will say to me on that day, 'Lord, Lord, **did we not prophesy in your name**, and in your name drive out demons and perform many miracles?' [23]Then I will tell them plainly, **'I never knew you. Away from me, you evildoers!'**"

This is a sad verse. Apparently when Jesus comes back, there will be many who think they are followers of Christ but will instead be told they are evildoers. They think they are shoo-ins because of their claim to prophecy and perform miracles, but Christ plainly tells them He never knew them. So be careful about placing your faith in modern-day prophets. There is no future in them.

Evangelist

Evangelist comes from the Greek word *euanggelisths*. This word means proclaimer of good tidings, or simply Preacher of the Gospel, someone who proclaims (herald of) the gospel to large groups in public places. So in today's church, the evangelist could be classified as the pulpit preacher.

There are at least two examples of evangelists in the New Testament, Timothy and Philip.

- 2 Timothy 4:5 But you, keep your head in all situations, endure hardship, do the work of an **evangelist**.
- Acts 21:8 Leaving the next day, we reached Caesarea and stayed at the house of Philip the **evangelist**, one of the Seven.

Responsibility

We can see that there are people doing the job of an evangelist in the New Testament, but what are the job requirements? Paul goes on to tell Timothy what those requirements are.

2 Timothy 4: 1-2 I give you this charge: [2]Preach the Word; be prepared in season and out of season; correct, rebuke and encourage—with great patience and careful instruction.

An evangelist is to preach from the Bible. The Bible is to be the basis for all of his lessons. He is to be prepared at all times. There is a similar reference to being prepared in 1 Peter 3:15.

1 Peter 3:15 Always be prepared to give an answer to everyone who asks you to give the reason for the hope that you have.

A preacher needs to be able to tell people about Christ, whether he is standing in front of a group or standing at the grocery checkout line. A preacher is to correct, rebuke, and encourage. These three words are held together with an "and" conjunction. This means they have equal importance. A preacher must be sure that he does all three. All too often a preacher will spend time correcting and rebuking but leave out encouragement, or maybe he will speak on encouragement and never spend time correcting. An evangelist cannot choose which one of these actions to practice. He must work to do all three. The ability to correct and rebuke without alienating a person can only be done with great patience and careful instruction. Rarely does someone want to be told they are doing something wrong. However, the job of an evangelist is to preach the truth that hits the mark without humiliating the member.

Checklist

One of my work functions has to do with developing checklists to measure a person's progress and development in a particular position. I have found that building a checklist is very difficult. Most people don't like to be graded, especially when they think they can do a job that they are not qualified to do. I used to take a pretty light attitude toward checklists until my boss told me the following: "If you give a person the OK and they are unable to perform the job, I will not hold that person responsible, I will hold you responsible." Once I found out I was graded, based on how well I placed people, I took the idea of a checklist much more seriously.

As I read the passage in 2 Timothy, related to the function of an evangelist, the idea of a checklist came to mind. We can summarize the requirements for an evangelist with this checklist:

- ☑ Preach the word.
- ☑ Be prepared in season and out of season.
- ☑ Correct.
- ☑ Rebuke.
- ☑ Encourage.
- ☑ Great patience.
- ☑ Careful instruction.

This checklist is not to be used to judge, but rather to ensure that the person who takes on the job of evangelist realizes what he is supposed to do. I did not create this checklist, God did. As a result, when we watch a preacher on television, in our home church, or at churches we visit, we should mentally evaluate their message according to these guidelines.

When I was a teenager, my friend's dad was a preacher at a church that was different than the one I was attending. I once asked my friend's dad why their church was doing certain things that were different than how I had been taught. I was not trying to be smart; I was just asking a question. The preacher responded to me with the following statement, "Our church does not feel that concept is important, so we do not discuss it or even bring it up." To this day, I am still taken back by this response. His response was not based on Scripture, it did not come with patience, and there was no instruction. Yet he felt justified in his answer.

Avoiding the question does not make the question go away.

Pastor (Elder)

The term pastor is derived from the Greek word *poimn*. This term means shepherd, one who looks after and cares for others. The term has the same meaning and is interchangeable with any of the following titles: Bishop, Presbyters, Guardians, Shepherds, Overseer (*episkopos*), Elder (*presbuteros*).

Responsibility

The person who holds this position has a big job in the local church. In 1 Peter 5:1-4 and 1 Timothy 5:17 that elders are the ones in charge of a local church. These passages show us that an elder can have multiple jobs in the church, but the primary function is to direct the affairs of the church. In Hebrews we see that the members of the church are to submit to their authority.

> Hebrews 13:17 [17]Obey your leaders and **submit to their authority**. They keep watch over you as men who must give an account. Obey them so that their work will be a joy, not a burden, for that would be of no advantage to you.

We also see how the term shepherd fits as well. A shepherd who looks over a flock of sheep takes care of that flock. The shepherd makes sure no lions or tigers are on the fringe and they make sure that sick members get the care they need. In Hebrews we see that the leader is one who keeps watch over the church. We also see the awesome responsibility of this position. The leader is to give an account for the members. If a member falls away, I can see the Lord asking the elder on the day of judgment, "What happened to this lost sheep?"

Requirements

The magnitude of the job of overseer is tremendous. As a result, it is important to have someone in that position worthy of the responsibility. Fortunately, we have been given two accounts of the job qualifications. These requirements are detailed in the following scriptures:

> Titus 1:6-7 [6]An **elder must** be blameless, the husband of but one wife, a man whose children believe and are not open to the charge of being wild and disobedient. [7]Since an **overseer** is entrusted with God's work, he must be blameless—not overbearing, not quick-tempered, not given to drunkenness, not violent, not pursuing dishonest gain.

Notice how elder and overseer are used interchangeably in this passage. In 1 Timothy, we see more detail on what the overseer is supposed to be.

> 1 Timothy 3: 1-7 [1]Here is a trustworthy saying: If anyone sets his heart on being an **overseer**, he desires a noble task. [2]Now the **overseer must** be above reproach, the husband of but one wife, temperate, self-controlled,

respectable, hospitable, able to teach, [3]not given to drunkenness, not violent but gentle, not quarrelsome, not a lover of money. [4]He must manage his own family well and see that his children obey him with proper respect. [5](If anyone does not know how to manage his own family, how can he take care of God's church?) [6]He must not be a recent convert, or he may become conceited and fall under the same judgment as the devil. [7]He must also have a good reputation with outsiders, so that he will not fall into disgrace and into the devil's trap.

Checklist

This person has quite a job. Converting these passages into a checklist looks like the following:

- ☑ Husband of but one wife.
- ☑ He must manage his own family well.
- ☑ Have his children obey him with proper respect.
- ☑ A man whose children believe.
- ☑ A man whose children are not wild and disobedient.
- ☑ Blameless.
- ☑ Must be above reproach.
- ☑ Must have a good reputation with outsiders.
- ☑ Respectable.
- ☑ Hospitable.
- ☑ Able to teach.
- ☑ Temperate.
- ☑ Self-controlled.
- ☑ Not overbearing.
- ☑ Not quick-tempered.
- ☑ Not given to drunkenness.
- ☑ Not violent.
- ☑ Not pursuing dishonest gain.
- ☑ Not violent but gentle.
- ☑ Not quarrelsome.
- ☑ Not a lover of money.
- ☑ He must not be a recent convert.

People say these requirements are unrealistic. When I hear this, I want to introduce them to my mom and dad. My dad, with the support of a super wife, was an elder for over 25 years.

Deacon

Deacon comes from the Greek word *diakonos.* The term means servant or minister performing a specific task. There are typically several deacons in a local congregation.

Responsibilities

They are often in charge of areas such as building and grounds, benevolence, missions, education, fellowship, etc. Any place that an elder sees a need for someone to watch over and be in charge is an area to which a deacon can be assigned.

Requirements

Their job requirements are clearly defined in the following passage:

1 Timothy 3: 8-13 [8]**Deacons**, likewise, are to be men worthy of respect, sincere, not indulging in much wine, and not pursuing dishonest gain. [9]They must keep hold of the deep truths of the faith with a clear conscience. [10]They must first be tested; and then if there is nothing against them, let them serve as deacons.

[11]In the same way, their wives are to be women worthy of respect, not malicious talkers but temperate and trustworthy in everything.

[12]A deacon must be the husband of but one wife and must manage his children and his household well. [13]Those who have served well gain an excellent standing and great assurance in their faith in Christ Jesus.

Checklist

We can summarize the requirements for a deacon with the following checklist.

- ☑ A man.
- ☑ Worthy of respect.
- ☑ Sincere.
- ☑ Not indulging in much wine.
- ☑ Not pursuing dishonest gain.
- ☑ Keeps hold of the deep truths of the faith with a clear conscience.
- ☑ Must first be tested, and then if there is nothing against him, let him serve as a deacon.
- ☑ Their wives are to be women worthy of respect.
- ☑ Their wives are not malicious talkers.
- ☑ Their wives are to be temperate and trustworthy in everything.
- ☑ Husband of one wife.
- ☑ Must manage his children and his household well.

Teachers

The term teacher comes from the Greek word *didaskalos*. The term means instructor.

Responsibilities

The job of a teacher is very important and it comes with a warning.

> James 3:1 Not many of you should presume to be teachers, my brothers, because you know that **we who teach will be judged more strictly**.

The position of teacher involves instructing people about the ways of the Lord. If a teacher is not grounded properly, the information that is taught can lead people down the wrong path. In my industry, I was an instructor. If I taught people to disregard safety, then people could be hurt or even killed. In the church, if an instructor does not respect the word of God, then the consequences can be eternal.

Requirements

The requirements for a teacher are given, based on what the instructor is to teach. These requirements are found in several different scriptures. Some of the more common scriptures dedicated to instruction are as follows:

- Matthew 28:18-20 [18]Then Jesus came to them and said, "All authority in heaven and on earth has been given to me. [19]Therefore go and make disciples of all nations, baptizing them in the name of the Father and of the Son and of the Holy Spirit, [20]and **teaching them to obey everything I have commanded you**. And surely I am with you always, to the very end of the age."
- Titus 2:1 You must teach what is in accord with sound doctrine.
- 1 Timothy 4:11 Command and **teach these things**.

From these passages, we see that a teacher is to teach the truth of God's Word. The next two passages give us guidelines concerning who can teach.

- 1 Timothy 2:12 [12]I do not permit a woman to teach or to have authority over a man; she must be silent.
- Titus 2:1-9 [1]You must **teach** what is in accord with **sound doctrine**. [2]**Teach** the **older men** to be temperate, worthy of respect, self-controlled, and sound in faith, in love and in endurance. [3]Likewise, **teach the older women** to be reverent in the way they live, not to be slanderers or addicted to much wine, but to **teach** what is good. [4]Then they can train the **younger women** to love their husbands and children, [5]to be self-controlled and pure, to be busy at home, to be kind, and to be subject to their husbands, so that no one will malign the word of God. [6]Similarly, **encourage** the **young men** to be self-controlled. [7]In everything set them an example by doing what is good. In your

teaching show integrity, seriousness [8]and soundness of speech that cannot be condemned, so that those who oppose you may be ashamed because they have nothing bad to say about us.   [9]**Teach slaves** to be subject to their masters in everything, to try to please them, not to talk back to them, [10]and not to steal from them, but to show that they can be fully trusted, so that in every way they will make the **teaching** about God our Savior attractive.

The passages in 1Timothy and Titus appear to contradict each other at first glance. In Timothy, we are told that a woman is not to teach. Then in Titus we see that older women are to teach. If we look at the full passage in 1 Timothy 2:12, we see that women are not to have authority over a man. This passage is another reference to the authority structure laid out in Ephesians 5:23 and 1 Corinthians 11:3. Just as a man is not to assume authority over Christ, a woman is not to assume authority over a man. This authority structure is not saying that women cannot teach. We see in Titus that older women are to teach the younger women, just not a man. A teacher is supposed to teach older men, younger men, older women, younger women, and slaves.   These five groups make up everyone. Teachers are to teach everyone.

Checklist

In light of these scriptures relating to teaching, we can summarize the requirements for a teacher with the following checklist:

- ☑ Teach the Scriptures to others.
- ☑ Walk the talk.
- ☑ Train people to be like Christ.
- ☑ Make the teaching of God attractive.
- ☑ Teach: older men, younger men, older women, younger women, and slaves.
- ☑ Women are not to teach men.

Teaching is a job we should all strive for. One of the reasons I like to teach is that teaching requires me to spend time in the Scriptures. I find that one of the best ways to learn a subject is to teach it.

Romans 2:21 you, then, who **teach** others, do you not **teach** yourself?

Closing Comments

The Bible says that Christ gave some to have leadership positions in the **Church that Christ built**. Christ is still in control today, and He will make sure that His church has solid leaders. Our job is to learn about these positions and to make sure we adhere to them. As we grow in our understanding of Christ's purpose for His church, we must not strive for leadership positions for the sake of having the position. Rather, we must find leaders who are qualified to prepare God's people for works of service. Christ was very particular about names and titles. He warns people in Matthew 23:1-13 about taking on a title rather than a job. In this passage, we see Christ scolding the Pharisees for letting people refer to them as Rabbi, father, and teacher. The Pharisees were the keepers of the Law of Moses and they enforced that law. However, in verses 3 and 5 we see that they were forcing people to obey them rather than the word of God. They liked being called by titles that elevated themselves above others. This is not the type of leader Christ wants. In verse 12 the Lord says leaders that operate in this fashion will be humbled.

In 3rd John 1:9 we read of an example of a church leader, Diotrephes, who had fallen into the same trap as the Pharisees. Some believe Diotrephes was an elder in the early church. His problem is one we have to work to avoid. Diotrephes had allowed his leadership position to go to his head. He was the one doing the enforcing rather than enforcing the word of God. He liked being in charge and being first. As a result, he was going down a path that was leading Christians away from the church. Christ gave some to be leaders in His church to bring people into the Kingdom, not the other way around. We should all look over the checklists defined in this section to make sure we are not falling into a trap that could lead people away from Christ.

I once read a publication related to the qualifications of church leaders. They term qualification was crossed out and replaced with the word suggestion. This is dangerous. All Scripture is God-breathed, and we cannot decide to pick and choose what verses we will follow. Our job is to follow what is written.

Questions to Consider
1. What is in a name?
2. Do titles match job descriptions?
3. How do the jobs and titles used in your church compare with the qualifications described in this chapter?
4. How are the jobs of an elder and a sheepherder similar?
5. Look at Titus 2:1-10 and define checklists for the assembly related to: Older Men, Younger Men, Older Women, Younger Women, and Slaves.
6. Is there ever a time when these checklists should not apply to the title they define?
7. In the King James version, what popular term used in the world of religion is only found in Psalms 111:9 to describe God.

Chapter 10: Who's in Charge?

Levels of Authority

The Bible is rich with mental imagery that tells us Christ is the head of His church and that His body is made alive by the actions of His church.

> Ephesians 1:22-23 [22]And God placed all things under his feet and appointed him to be **head over everything for the church,** [23]**which is his body**, the fullness of him who fills everything in every way.

A body cannot live or make decisions without the head. Since Christ is the head of His church, we, His body, are subject to the direction of Christ. Few religious organizations will debate this fact. However, the interaction within the body has raised considerable confusion as well as religious division. In the last chapter we looked at the different leadership positions found in the body and we defined the responsibilities for each position. In this chapter, we will be looking at how the different parts of the body are to interact not only with each other, but also with other churches.

Double Honor

As the New Testament Christians continued to grow, churches were being started all over the countryside. In nearly every case, we see the mention of elders when the church is mentioned.

- Acts 14:23 Paul and Barnabas appointed elders for them in **each church**.
- Philemon 1:1 Paul and Timothy, servants of Christ Jesus, To all the saints in Christ Jesus at Philippi, together with the **overseers (bishops)** and **deacons**.
- Titus 1:5 To Titus, Paul said, "The reason I left you in Crete was that you might straighten out what was left unfinished and appoint **elders** in every town, as I directed you."
- Acts 20: 17, 28 Paul told the **elders of the church in Ephesus** to "Keep watch over yourselves and all the flock of which the Holy Spirit has made you overseers. Be shepherds of the church of God, which he bought with his own blood."

In these examples, we conclude that the elders of a church have a big job. In Acts 20, the elders are to keep watch over the body as a shepherd keeps watch over a flock. The position of elder is not to be taken lightly or to be taken alone. In all of these examples, we never hear of a single elder presiding over the body of a local church. These references talk about elders, not an elder.

Elders are not only responsible for the members' souls, they are also responsible for all the affairs of the Church.

> 1 Timothy 5:17 The **elders** who **direct the affairs** of the church well are worthy of **double honor**, especially those whose work is **preaching and teaching**.

As members we need to respect the position and man who holds the title of elder. There is no way we can know all that an elder has to do. However, I was the son of one for over 25 years. I cannot tell you the number of times my dad missed dinner because of emergency phone calls, trips to the hospital, or late night meetings at the building. The job of an elder is demanding, but I never heard my father complain. Remember that an elder is compared to a shepherd. This is no coincidence. A shepherd's job is to make sure the flock is safe, healthy, and has good food to eat. Elders are to make sure the body of Christ is safe, growing strong, and eating the correct spiritual food. We need to say thanks to our elders and do our best to strengthen them so that they don't get discouraged.

> Hebrews 13:17 **Obey your leaders** and **submit to their authority**. **They keep watch over you** as **men who must give an account**. **Obey them** so that their work **will be a joy**, **not a burden**, for that would be of no advantage to you.

The Hebrew writer echoes our need to appreciate our leaders. After all, they are to keep watch over us and be prepared to give an account. The elders have to explain to God someday why a member has fallen away. If you owned a herd of sheep and your shepherd came back with 5 less than he left with, don't you think you would want to know what happened to them? Of course you would. The same is true of God. He wants the body of Christ to stay strong. If the body is falling apart, Christ is going to want to know what happened and He will be asking the elders. We also see in this verse that the body is to obey and submit to the authority of the elders. Unfortunately, sometimes decisions made by elders can cause bad feelings among the members. We as members need to realize that we do not see the same picture that the elders see. If an elder comes to us and tells us he is concerned about some portion of our life, we need to listen to his warning. In fact, we should be eager to follow his guidance. Our job is to make the elders' job easier.

The interaction of Christ, elders, and the other members of the body has been illustrated in the following figure.

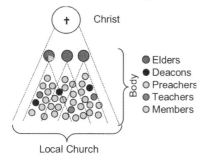

Christ is the head of His body and He is in charge. The body of Christ is made up of many parts and these parts include elders. The elders are in charge of the local body of Christ. We must realize and appreciate the parts of the body are subject not only to Christ, but also to the leadership, guidance, and direction of the elders.

Figure 13: Christ and His body

One Another

As I was teaching a class related to the interactions between older and younger members, one of the members of the class asked if it would be OK to ask an older member to evaluate how they were doing as a Christian. I thought for a minute and said I wish we all could be proactive in our self-evaluation rather than reactive. Why should we wait to fail if we can be told of a potential roadblock in our path? Why not steer around it before we plow head on into an avoidable problem?

The New Testament is full of passages that tell us to be devoted to each other. A few of them are listed here:

- Ephesians 5:21 **Submit to one another** out of reverence for Christ.
- Romans 12:10 **Be devoted to one another** in brotherly love. Honor one another above yourselves.
- Galatians 6:1-2 [1]Brothers, if someone is caught in a sin, you who are spiritual should restore him **gently**. But watch yourself, or you also may be tempted. [2]**Carry each other's burdens**, and in this way you will fulfill the law of Christ.

The levels of authority start with Christ, moves to elders, and stops with each of us. The arrangement that Christ set up requires each of us to take care of the rest. We have to first examine ourselves to make sure we don't have a log in our eye when trying to get a speck of dust out of our brother's eye. In Matthew 18, we are told how to go about restoring a brother who has slipped.

Matthew 18:15-17 [15]"If your brother sins against you, go and show him his fault, **just between the two of you**. If he listens to you, you have won your brother over. [16]But if he will not listen, take **one or two others along**, so that 'every matter may be established by the testimony of two or three witnesses.' [17]If he refuses to listen to them, tell it **to the church**; and if he refuses to listen even to the church, treat him as you would a pagan or a tax collector."

This passage, along with the others related to brotherly love, indicates that we all have a responsibility toward each other. Falling away from Christ should be difficult. We should not be resentful when a brother points out a potential flaw. We should be thankful for the concern. We are to watch out for each other so that we can all make it to heaven.

Generation Gap
Keeping watch over each other is easy to say, but difficult to apply. The easy road to take when we see a brother slipping is to look away. However, that is not how brotherly love works. In this section, we will examine a few examples of how we can all learn not only from each other but especially from our older members.

In Titus, chapter 2, we read of the responsibilities regarding the training relationship between older and younger members of the body of Christ. This relationship acts as a bridge for the generation gap. We see that the older members are to teach the younger members. Those who have traveled further on the road of life often have a life perspective that does not come from books. The training relationship taught in Titus implies that the younger members should be looking for and expecting instruction from those with more experience.

Young families should be seeking counsel from members who have successfully raised Christian children or worked through particularly difficult situations. The older members of a congregation have a wealth of real-world experience related to being a Christian. Many have been dedicated to Christ for decades. That dedication has developed and strengthened a faith that younger members need to respect.

However, getting involved can be a challenge. The other day a few young kids were running through the building. I told them to walk and then realized I was getting old. Actually, when I saw those kids, I looked down at the scar on my hand. You see, when I was their age I had been running in the same hall and in the same way. I wish someone had told me to walk because I ran into a metal edge on a chalkboard and slit my hand open. I felt awkward asking these young kids to walk, and they thought I was being unfair, but they left the building with no blood loss.

A few years ago, we had a group of young kids who liked to play in the parking lot after worship. Later we found that they liked to hide under the cars. We took action, got the parents involved, and set restrictions on play areas. Can you imagine the potential for danger if you let a child hide under a car? Action had to be taken.

These examples may seem obvious, but there is a host of examples that get much more complicated. Consider this next one. An older couple is walking to their car after worship. They come across a teenage couple embraced in a very passionate lip lock. The older couple has to make a decision - do they walk on by or do they intervene? If they intervene, they run the risk of embarrassing the kids and upsetting their parents. What should they do? What would you do? Let's fill in the rest of the story. If we roll the clock back some 20 years, we see the older couple confronted with almost the same situation. At that time, they did not feel it was their job to counsel the young teens. After all, that was the parents' job. So they chose the path that walked around the situation. Unfortunately, shortly after their decision, the teens were pregnant. The older couple felt responsible for the outcome because they had not intervened earlier. This time around, their fear of ridicule and embarrassment was outweighed by the harsh reality of the potential road that lay ahead for these teens. So they chose the difficult path and intervened.

There are all kinds of examples of situations that require action. That action will either be to turn away or to intervene. I think this next example illustrates the folly of turning away. Suppose you are driving a car down a road and see a good friend waving nicely at you. You would probably smile and wave back. That is, until the next turn when you smash into the sinkhole your friend's car is in. Next you climb out of the sinkhole and chase your friend down to ask them why he did not warn you of the danger ahead. Your friend looks at you in an odd sort of way and then tells you he did not want to bother you or cause you alarm. At that point, you may start to question the type of friend you have.

The road of life is full of holes that we can fall in. What better way to find those holes than to ask people who have been down these roads before us? Many of our older members have either been down the same road or have seen the outcome of people who have taken the wrong path. We need to seek their advice so we limit the risk of falling into the same holes.

The World's Safety Net
So far we have seen that the members of the body of Christ are to submit to each other as well as to the authority of the elders. We also see that Christ is still in charge. If we examine these relationships more closely, we see that the head is connected directly to the body. Notice in all the scriptures referenced earlier that elders were to keep watch over their flock, not flocks. In fact, we can find no place in Scripture where multiple churches were subject to the same group of elders. In Timothy, we get a glimpse of how different churches are to interact.

2 Timothy 2: 1-6 [1]You then, my son, be strong in the grace that is in Christ Jesus. [2]And the things you have heard me say in the presence of many witnesses entrust to reliable men who will also be qualified to teach others. [3]Endure hardship with us like a good soldier of Christ Jesus. **[4]No one serving as a soldier gets involved in civilian affairs**—he wants to please his commanding officer. [5]Similarly, if anyone competes as an athlete, he does not receive the victor's crown unless he competes according to the rules. [6]The hardworking farmer should be the first to receive a share of the crops.

In this passage, a soldier, a commanding officer, and a civilian are used to show the interaction of authority in **the Church that Christ Built**. In the military world, a soldier only carries out orders passed on to him from his commanding officer. He is not to listen to orders from anyone else. In addition, he is only to worry about what his commanding officer thinks, carrying out those orders with the support of his fellow soldiers. A soldier who concerns himself with actions unrelated to his orders will be distracted from those orders. In the same way, the ultimate commanding officer of the global church is Christ Himself. We are all subject to Christ and Christ is making sure His church is being taken care of. Christ set up the local churches to be pockets of light in their communities. These local churches are to be self-governed by only their elders. In this way, the commanding officers of the local church are the elders. Members of the local body need not worry about what other churches or even what other members are doing. Christ makes sure that local churches are being started, elders make sure that local church members are being equipped to do good works, and members need only to focus on doing good works so that the body can more clearly reflect Christ. This is such a simple plan and one that shows the brilliance of Christ. In this way, **the Church that Christ built** can actually span the globe and even act as the world's safety net.

The plan that Christ set up is so simple. However, it gets so messed up. Take, for example, a story my father-in-law told me. Before his retirement, he was a manager of several crews for the phone company. He told me that one of his biggest problems was keeping his guys focused on the task they were given. Inevitably one of the groups would take notice of another group that was not doing its job properly. This group would then complain to my father-in-law. They thought they were doing a good job by letting him know of this other group's poor workmanship. However, they were not focused on finishing their own task and were unable to finish on time. Something my father-in-law said stuck with me. He said that if his crews would just do the jobs he assigned and let him worry about what crew was not working, his job would have been much easier and his team would have been much more productive. This example is so common, not only in the workforce but also amongst our church family. If all of the members of the body could focus on doing good works rather than on who is getting credit for those works, or what problems the church down the road is having, then the light of Christ could shine so much brighter.

Scripture is not silent with regards to the organization structures associated with **the Church that Christ built.** There are fundamentally two types of structures that religious organizations use today: Single Layer and Multi-Layered structures. By comparing these layers to Biblical examples, we can determine what our Lord has in mind.

Single Layered Structure

When we look at the structure of Christ in the light of this discussion, the structure would look as follows:

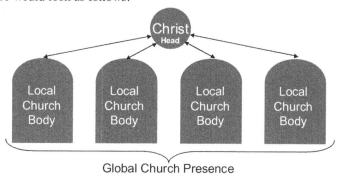

Global Church Presence

Figure 14: Globally owned, Locally operated

I happen to work for a global company. One of our phrases over the years was "Globally owned, locally operated." The idea was that the local groups could better adapt to the needs of the local territory. However, we had a set of global resources that would allow us to solve any problem that a client might come across. This is a pretty powerful saying and one that when implemented correctly is hard to beat. Christ knew the power of this type of organization. He knows that the brightest light for a community is a light in that community. Christ is in control and He will see to it that His body is cared for properly. After all, the Bible does tell us that He knows who are His.

2 Timothy 2:19 The Lord knows those who are his.

Multi-Layered Structure

I mentioned that the company I work for is a global company. In order for it to run properly, our president has several vice presidents. Each VP is over a country. The country is further divided into sections based on customer base. Each section of the company then has a senior manager. The different sections are then further divided based on industry types. So by the time I get to my manager, there are several layers between the president and myself. This structure in business is not uncommon or even new. Multi-layered management business models have been around forever. As a result of the natural need for this type of business management, many have felt the need to set up a similar structure within the church.

An example of how a multi-layered structure may be applied to churches is as follows. Assume there are several churches in your town. A few questions come to mind. If the churches don't talk to each other, then how can we be sure that not all the churches are supporting the exact same function, leaving other functions in the community unattended? How would we know what each church is doing? How could we be sure that the needs of the community are being met properly? These seem like valid questions that can be answered by simply adding a layer of management to ensure that the area churches are not overlapping. Now that that problem is solved, what happens if we move up to the state level? We now see that a level of management would be needed to ensure that the state is covered properly from a religious perspective. OK then, now that each state has a religious manager, it would only be natural to have a country manager. The progression would continue upward until there was a single point of contact that made sure the entire church was working according to Christ's plan. This form of religious government would have the following flow chart.

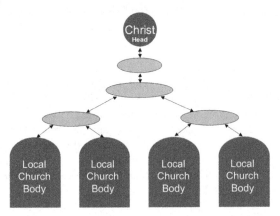

Figure 15: Multi-Level Government

This structure seems logical as well as common. This type of structure is the way corporate business, the military, school systems, and just about anything that involves people and money is governed.

Structure Comparison

As hard as a person tries to make an argument concerning the multi-layered church government, we cannot find any examples in Scripture where this church structure is justified. The problem with this type of structure is that it takes Christ out of the picture. The flaw in the multi-level structure logic is that **the Church that Christ Built** is not a man-made organization. Christ's church is a divine organization. The multiple levels added between Christ and His body actually show our lack of faith in Christ's ability to manage His body. Does man know better than Christ what the body should do? Christ is in control. Christ does not need the extra levels of management.

Church Structure Evolution

The single-versus-multiple church government structure is a controversial topic in our religious world today. Fundamentally, the two different viewpoints stem from how the following picture is interpreted.

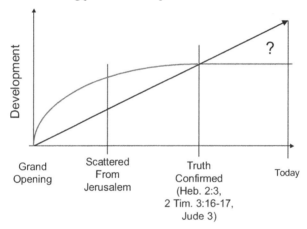

Figure 16: Structure Evolution

In this figure there are two lines. Each line represents a view related to church government. Both groups will agree that the church started on the day of Pentecost and that it was scattered from Jerusalem when Stephen was stoned. However, this is where the agreement usually stops. The line that keeps going up represents the view taken by the multi-layered group. Their belief looks at the development of the church as simply a natural evolution of the first-century church. They feel that the growth of the church requires additional levels of management to ensure the message of Christ is consistent. The line that starts up fast and then levels off represents the belief of the single-layered group. They believe that the structure of **the Church that Christ built** was defined by the close of the Scriptures. They believe no additional levels are needed because these levels cannot be found in Scripture.

This is an interesting problem and one that is not easily solved. This problem further emphasizes the issue relating to the silence of the Scripture being prohibitive or permissive. Let's take a look at one of the warnings from Paul concerning problems that would soon face the early church.

> Acts 20:28-30 [28]Keep watch over yourselves and all the flock of which the Holy Spirit has made you overseers. Be shepherds of the church of God, which he bought with his own blood. [29]I know that after I leave, **savage wolves will come in among you** and will not spare the flock. [30]Even from **your own number men** will arise and **distort the truth** in order to draw away disciples after them.

Paul was telling the church leaders to be on their guard. He knew that soon men from their own congregation would rise up and distort the truth. When we use the Bible as our guide, we cannot find justification for any of the following examples:

- An elder being exalted above another.
- The term Bishop being used to identify an office other than an elder.
- One person, other than Christ, given authority over local churches.

In fact, we find quite the opposite in scripture. We are warned about those who felt they had the same authority as scripture, the apostles, or even Christ Himself. As a result, "new" religious laws and practices are being introduced to keep up with what men "think" God wants. As logical as these progressions seem, if they are not supported by Scripture, we must resist. These "improvements" represent human additions made to help out a divine institution. The problem with that statement is that divine institutions don't need human additions to run better. Christ is the master builder and He defined His Church to help us get to heaven. If we could just follow His simple plan, we would change the world!

Coincidence or Providence?

Good intentions are one of the biggest reasons multi-layered religious structures were developed. People want to make sure a community is properly covered from a needs perspective. The problem is that people cannot know all the needs, no matter how hard they try. God is the only one who knows our needs. He will see to it that His church is working in the appropriate area. The following passage further illustrates that God knows what our needs are.

> Matthew 6:30-34 O you of little faith? [31]So do not worry, saying, 'What shall we eat?' or 'What shall we drink?' or 'What shall we wear?' [32]For the pagans run after all these things, and **your heavenly Father knows that you need them.** [33]But seek first his kingdom and his righteousness, and all these things will be given to you as well. [34]Therefore do not worry about tomorrow, for tomorrow will worry about itself. Each day has enough trouble of its own.

We have to have faith that Christ will direct His body. Still, as humans we would like to understand how He does this. The answer is found in faith. Knowing exactly how He keeps His church moving is not something we can understand and should not be something we concern ourselves with. This is easy to say, but hard to do. I am not qualified to define how Christ works today. In fact, no one is. I am sure that many of our life's experiences have been credited to a coincidence when actually they should be credited to the providence of God.

I have had several opportunities to see the brilliance of Christ's plan with my travels around the world. I mentioned my trip to France and our relationship with the missionaries there a few chapters back. What I did not mention is that they lost some of their support shortly after I visited them. I took their situation to the leaders of the church we were attending and explained what they needed. The fellowship of believers now helps support them. Many will chalk this up to coincidence. Maybe so, but I like to think I was an instrument being used by Christ to help out a brother in need. Things like this happen all the time. We have been so tuned to believe that Christ is no longer taking an active role as the Head of His church that we all too often mistake His hand for a coincidence. Our job is to let Christ care for His body, let the elders care about their flock, and let us be concerned with doing the work of the Lord.

> Micah 6:8 He has shown you, O mortal, what is good. And what does the LORD require of you? To act justly and to love mercy and to walk humbly with your God.

Simple . . .

Questions to Consider

1. What are examples of items used in our daily life that have stopped evolving?
2. How can we make sure that our religious practices are consistent with what God wants?
3. When is it appropriate for one group of elders to provide leadership support for another church?
4. What attitude should we have when on the receiving end of correction?
5. What are ways we can make the job of the elder easier?
6. Name several examples of how God's providence has made sure that His work gets done.
7. Read the story of Joseph in the Old Testament and ask yourself if his journey were coincidence or providence?
8. Read Revelation 19:11-21. Does the image of that rider indicate a need for help? Match this image to Christ as the leader and His army as His Church. Then ask yourself how a human can improve the plan.

Chapter 11: Mission

Mission

Impossible

I used to watch the old television show *Mission Impossible*. In those shows, a seemingly impossible mission is assigned to the lead agent. The mission is usually given on an electronic device (M*ission Impossible* theme song in the background). At the end of each message you hear the phrase, "This is your mission should you choose to accept it. This message will self-destruct in 10 seconds." Then the message disintegrates. I have never known the agent to turn down the mission.

There is something about having a mission that fuels the desire to act. Can you imagine a life with no mission? Our missions may not self-destruct, but they can come in all kinds of forms. For example, when my wife gives me a grocery list, I can almost hear the *Mission Impossible* theme song in the background. I take that list and I don't come home until I have purchased every item. At work, we frequently hear about mission statements all the time. An example of could be, "We will surpass our customer's expectations" or "Quality is job one." These statements are intended to provide the underlying theme that the entire company works toward.

Mission statements are not bad. In fact, they are good things. Not having a mission statement can result in poor performance. The phrase, "Idle hands are the devil's play things" comes to mind when I hear people say they don't need a mission statement. I have a little dog that is the best thing when we are home. However when we leave, he transforms into a little sneak. He knows he is not allowed to have a treat unless he does something good, but he really likes his treats. On one occasion when we came home, we could not find his treat dish. I found it several days later underneath an end table. He had gotten it off the shelf and tried to open it. We could see the teeth marks in the plastic. He must have tried for a while, but when he failed, he hid it. Sometimes people and puppies are not much different. If we do not have clear objectives, we can get ourselves into trouble. Just try to go on a diet without keeping track of what you eat, or try to save money without a budget, or try reading your Bible without a daily plan. All of these things are virtually impossible without a clearly defined mission coupled with a clear plan.

Up to this point, we have talked about how to recognize the framework of Christ's church. However, recognizing Christ's church alone will not fulfill the mission of **the Church that Christ Built**. Sure, worshiping with the right mind set, enjoying each other's company, properly recognizing leadership positions, and understanding worship woes are all crucial and important religious tasks.

However if we focus only on these tasks, our worship will be in vain. After all, what good is a perfect part if it stays in a box? What good is the perfect cake if no one eats it? What good is a light if it is kept under a bushel? I like to go to garage sales to find little treasures. On one occasion I purchased a Lionel 1963 train set in near perfect condition. The train had never been taken out of the box. I took the train to a dealer and it was appraised for 10 times what I paid for it. I eventually traded it for slot cars at a value of almost 30 times what I paid. This was a good find, but when I had the train appraised the toy specialist said, "It is a shame the train was never used as it was intended to be used." How interesting. We can have the best looking worship, but if we fail to use the church as Christ intended, then our mechanism of worship has failed. Christ did not design the perfect church so that it could be kept in a box for safekeeping. He designed His church for a specific purpose. That purpose can be found in the mission statement used by **the Church that Christ built**.

Statement

In the last chapter, we reviewed the functional description of the church as it is defined in Ephesians.

> Ephesians 4:11-13 [11]It was he (Christ) who gave some to be apostles, some to be prophets, some to be evangelists, and some to be pastors and teachers, [12]to prepare God's people for **works of service**, so that the body of Christ may be built up [13]until we reach unity in the faith and in the knowledge of the Son of God and become mature, attaining to the whole measure of the fullness of Christ.

We used this passage to identify the leadership positions in Christ's church. However, if we look a little closer at verse 12, we can find the mission statement for **the Church that Christ Built**.

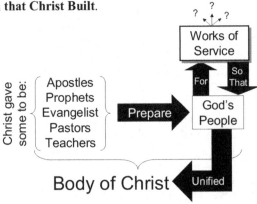

Figure 17: Functional Description

Christ's church prepares people for works of service. This seems over simplified, but sometimes the best plans are simple. Christ simply wants us to do works of service. The reason for us to do these works is so we can build up the body to look more like Christ. Remember that Christ is the Head of the church and the members of the church make up His body. Therefore, we should not be surprised that Christ would expect His body to reflect Him.

The question that comes up is: "What works of service are we to do?" This is a good question and one that can be answered by looking into the life of Christ. If we as the body of Christ are to reflect Him, then we as a body should study Him. The more we learn about Christ, the better we will be able to know what works of service are required of us.

Life of Christ

Mission

Christ lived among us for 33 years. We get to read a little about Him when He was a young boy, but then not again until He was nearly 30. We have only been given snapshots of our Savior while He was on earth. However, in those snapshots we get to see what type of person He was. He was driven with a passion that was greater than we can imagine. He knew He was only on earth for a short time, but He had a clear objective. He had a mission that we are told of in Luke.

Luke 19:10 For the Son of Man came to **seek and to save what was lost**.

Christ's job on earth was to establish a spiritual kingdom. He needed to set a plan in motion that would get as many people into the kingdom as possible. Everything Christ did was tied to His goal of seeking and saving the lost. Today we don't use the word seek very often. This word means to earnestly look for something. The emotion I feel when I realize I have misplaced my wallet, or when I think my child is in a certain place only to realize he is not where I thought he was. That feeling of panic, coupled with an unbelievable desire to find what was lost, comes close to how our Lord must have felt about finding and saving lost souls. His goal was clear, and His life's work shows the passion He had to fulfill His mission statement.

Action Plan

The mission of our Lord was clear, but how did He carry out his mission? What did He do that has resulted in the world knowing His name? In order to find out, we have to look into the Scriptures. In Matthew we see the formula Christ used during His ministry.

Matthew 9:35 (Matthew 4:23) Jesus went through all the towns and villages, **teaching** in their synagogues, **preaching** the good news of the kingdom and **healing** every disease and sickness.

This passage shows us that Christ mastered His mission by working in three primary areas: Teaching, preaching, and healing. Understanding how Christ worked in these areas will give us insights into the works of service Christ has in mind for His church to carry out.

Teaching

Christ was a great teacher. There are many verses in the New Testament where He was addressed simply as Teacher.

- Matthew 22:36 "**Teacher**, which is the greatest commandment in the Law?"
- Mark 4:38 Jesus was in the stern, sleeping on a cushion. The disciples woke him and said to him, "**Teacher**, don't you care if we drown?"

I hope that in heaven they have tape recordings of some of Christ's lessons. His ability to speak with authority, convey His point, and move people was nothing less than extraordinary. The Bible even tells us in several chapters how His words left people with a sense of amazement.

- Matthew 13:34 Coming to his hometown, he began **teaching** the people in their synagogue, and they were amazed. "Where did this man get this wisdom and these miraculous powers?" they asked.
- Mark 1:22 The people were amazed at his **teaching**, because he taught them as one who had authority, not as the teachers of the law.

Jesus never missed an opportunity to teach people. We see that He taught in synagogues, temple courts, in towns, and on riverbanks. He always was prepared, and He converted everyday moments into teachable moments.

- Matthew 11:1 After Jesus had finished instructing his twelve disciples, he went on from there to **teach** and preach in the towns of Galilee.
- Mark 2:3 Once again Jesus went out beside the lake. A large crowd came to him, and he began to **teach** them.
- Mark 6:7 Then Jesus went around **teaching** from village to village.
- Mark 14:49 Every day I was with you, **teaching** in the temple courts

Jesus was the master of the teachable moment. The New Testament is filled with examples where He made lessons out of everyday events such as getting a drink of water, watching people put money in a plate, a fruitless fig tree, eating lunch, a thunderstorm, going fishing, vineyards, and the list goes on and on. Jesus was known as Teacher for good reason. He did not miss an opportunity to teach, but what did He teach? The following passages give us insights into His lessons.

- Mark 6:34 So he began teaching them **many things**.
- Mark 8:31 He then began to **teach** them that the Son of Man must suffer many things and be rejected by the elders, chief priests and teachers of the law, and that he must be killed and after three days rise again.
- Mark 12:38 As he **taught**, Jesus said, "Watch out for the teachers of the law."
- Luke 10:25 "**Teacher**," he asked, "what must I do to inherit eternal life?"
- Luke 20:21 "**Teacher**, we know that you speak and **teach** what is right, and that you do not show partiality but **teach** the way of God in accordance with the truth."

These scriptures begin to give us a glimpse of what Christ taught. He taught whatever needed to be taught related to spiritual things. He taught about salvation, the spiritual kingdom He was building, how we should love one another, and about His death, burial, and resurrection. No matter what He taught, we can be sure that Christ only taught truth and He was not swayed by the opinions of men. The Lord is the ultimate teacher. In fact, we see in Matthew that if anyone tries to call themselves teacher in a way that would elevate themselves to the level of the Lord, that is a big problem.

Matthew 23:10 Nor are you to be called 'teacher,' for you have one **Teacher**, the Christ.

Preaching

Christ was not only an excellent teacher, He was a great preacher as well. As a teacher we see Him sitting with people, often in a question-and-answer format. As a preacher we see Him proclaiming a message. The following are a few of the passages that talk about Christ the preacher.

- Matthew 4:17 From that time on Jesus began to **preach**, "Repent, for the kingdom of heaven is near."
- Mark 1:14-15 [14]After John was put in prison, Jesus went into Galilee, **proclaiming** the **good news** of God. [15]"The time has come," he said. "The kingdom of God is near. Repent and believe the good news!"
- Mark 1:38 Jesus replied, "Let us go somewhere else—to the nearby villages—so I can **preach** there also. **That is why I have come**."
- Luke 8:1 After this, Jesus traveled about from one town and village to another, proclaiming the **good news** of the kingdom of God.

The message that often comes up when we hear of Christ as a preacher is the good news related to God, the gospel, and the kingdom of heaven being near. The kingdom of heaven is the church Christ was building. Have you ever made something neat and then wanted to show it to as many people as you could? I once built a car. When it was finally done, I drove it all over the place. I would find ways to bring up my car in conversations with my friends and with strangers. I even entered it into car shows and won a trophy. I loved that car, I wanted people to see it, and I wanted to talk about it. I am sure we have all done something we thought was neat and then wanted to tell people about it. Christ was no different. He was making His church come to life. He was setting a plan in place that is still active today. Christ was excited about His church and He told as many people as He could tell. I can almost see His face beam with pride as He proclaimed how awesome this kingdom would be. He could not have stopped telling people even if He tried.

Do we look at **the Church that Christ built** as being good news today? Seems that if Christ was so passionate about His Church, maybe we should study to learn what the good news is all about.

Caring
In addition to Christ being an excellent teacher and preacher, He was a kind, compassionate, caring man who healed people whenever He could. There are several passages where Christ healed people. A few are mentioned here:
- Matthew 11:5 The blind receive sight, the lame walk, those who have leprosy are cured, the deaf hear, the dead are raised, and the good news is preached to the poor.
- Matthew 14:14 When Jesus landed and saw a large crowd, he **had compassion** on them and **healed** their sick.
- Matthew 17:18 Jesus rebuked the demon, and it came out of the boy, and he was **healed** from that moment.
- Luke 6:17 A large crowd of his disciples was there and a great number of people from all over Judea, from Jerusalem, and from the coast of Tyre and Sidon, [18]who had come to hear him and to be **healed of their diseases**. Those troubled by evil spirits were cured, [19]and the people all tried to touch him, because power was coming from him and **healing them all**.
- Luke 9:6 So they set out and went from village to village, preaching the gospel and **healing** people everywhere.

There are so many examples in the New Testament of Christ taking care of people. This small list hardly does justice to the work of the Lord. However, from these few selected verses, it is easy to see that Christ took care of people's needs. He had an ability to heal that we don't have today, but we can have compassion, we can take care of the sick, we can look after the needy, we can send a card or visit someone in the hospital. No, we can't heal people by our presence, but a pat on the back or the touch of the hand can do wonders to raise the spirits of someone in need of a loving touch.

Winning Combination

Christ set out to seek and save the lost. He did it with a winning combination that included teaching, preaching, and caring for others. His three-point plan changed the world. The positive spin-offs of the works of the Lord included: Finding the lost, Caring for others, Being a light to the world, Building His church, Edifying others, Giving, Saving the lost, and Nurturing, to name a few.

Can the same winning combination be used today? Can we as Christians do works of service that include teaching, preaching, and caring for others? The answer is yes! Christ told us to follow His example. Through Mark he instructs us to preach the good news.

> Mark 16:15-16 [15]He said to them, "Go into all the world and **preach** the **good news** to all creation. [16]Whoever believes and is baptized will be saved, but whoever does not believe will be condemned."

He tells us in Matthew to obey all of his commands.

> Matthew 28:18-20 [18]Then Jesus came to them and said, "All authority in heaven and on earth has been given to me. [19]Therefore go and make disciples of all nations, baptizing them in the name of the Father and of the Son and of the Holy Spirit, [20]and teaching them **to obey everything I have commanded you**. And surely I am with you always, to the very end of the age."

In Ephesians we are reminded that we were created to do good works.

> Ephesians 2:10 For we are God's workmanship, created in Christ Jesus to do **good works**, which God prepared in advance for us to do.

In 1st Peter, Peter builds on the concept of doing good works to let us know we are to do them so that people will glorify God.

> 1 Peter 2:11-12 [11]Dear friends, I urge you, as aliens and strangers in the world, to abstain from sinful desires, which war against your soul. [12]**Live such good lives** among the pagans that, though they accuse you of doing wrong, they may see your **good deeds** and glorify God on the day he visits us.

James tells us that the religion God wants is one that has His people staying pure and caring for others.

> James 1:27 Religion that God our Father accepts as pure and faultless is this: to **look after orphans and widows** in their distress and to **keep oneself from being polluted by the world.**

Members of **the Church that Christ built** actively try to reflect the life of Christ by doing works of service that show the world that He is real and alive. These actions are not considered burdens. They are responsibilities for which we gladly volunteer ourselves.

> 1 Corinthians 12:12 The body is a unit, though it is made up of many parts; and though all its parts are many, they form one body. So it is with Christ.

Offices of the Church

Our works of service can be accomplished with the same combination used by Christ: Teaching, preaching, and caring. In fact, Christ set up His church to ensure that this combination would be carried out. Notice how well the works of service required of the church match the offices of the church that Christ defined.

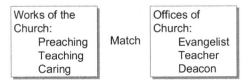

Figure 18: Works of Service vs Offices of the Church

There is no coincidence that Christ set up preachers, teachers, and deacons to ensure that works of service would get done.

Closing Comments

The Church that Christ built prepares its members to reflect Christ. This reflection shows up in everyday people applying the winning combination of teaching, preaching, and caring for others.

> Ephesians 4:16 [16]From him the whole body, joined and held together by every supporting ligament, grows and builds itself up in love, as each part does its work.

In this passage, we see that each part of Christ's church has a role to fill. Being part of the Church is not a spectator sport. Members are to be actively looking for ways to strengthen the body. We may not all be able to preach or teach in a formal way, but all of us can tell a friend about Christ. In fact, the good news of the gospel should motivate us to tell others about Him.

Matthew 10:31-32 "Whoever acknowledges me before men, I will also acknowledge him before my Father in heaven. [33]But whoever disowns me before men, I will disown him before my Father in heaven.

Not only should the body of Christ be looking for ways to acknowledge Him, we should continually be looking for ways to help others. We may not be able to prescribe medicine for the sick, but we can take food, send a card, or simply pray. Works of service are not a burden. They are actions that become as automatic as breathing. When the body of Christ works as a unit to continually serve, **the Church that Christ built** not only allows Christ to live, it brings glory to God and paves the way for people to get to heaven.

Matthew 5:16 In the same way, let your light shine before men, that they may see your good deeds and praise your Father in heaven.

The positive spin-offs for a healthy church body are endless. The following figure illustrates the possibilities resulting from a winning combination of preaching, teaching, and caring for others.

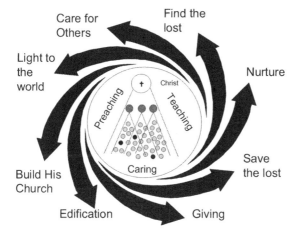

Figure 19: Endless Possibilities

The only reflection some people will ever see of Christ is what they see when they visit a congregation of believers. What reflection are they receiving? In a very real sense, churches that do not practice the works of service as defined by Him are showing a lifeless body of Christ.

Everett Ferguson said it best in the following quote:

> "When the church fails to do the work of Christ, it becomes the corpse instead of the body of Christ."

Christ is alive and well and can be clearly seen in the exciting, vibrant, and healthy **Church that Christ Built**.

Questions to Consider
1. What works of service can we do every day?
2. When was the last time you performed a work of service?
3. When you help someone, how does it make you feel?
4. How does doing works of service make us look more like Christ?
5. How is your church preparing you to help others?

Chapter 12: The Touch of the Master's Hand

Reflection

As I get older, time goes faster and faster. When I was a kid, summer vacation lasted forever. Hot summer days seemed to never end. Now that I have kids, if I blink a couple times I see my dad's reflection when I look in the mirror. How does that happen? It was just yesterday I got the call that my wife was about to give birth to our first child. In a few months my youngest starts college. Time flies. All my attempts to slow down time have failed, my kids are getting older, my forehead keeps getting bigger, and retirement is no longer a faint light on the horizon. Every once in awhile, I try to stop time and simply watch the world go by. Some call this reflection. I suppose that is a good description. Taking time to look back at your life can sometimes help you see where you are going.

As I take a moment to reflect on this book, I am amazed to find myself on the last chapter. This book became an idea several years ago when I was asked to teach a high school Bible class. The subject that was given to me was the subject of "church." As I prepared for that lesson, I noticed that the material focused more on the mechanics of worship as opposed to the intent of worship. I could not see where the mechanics of worship matched the good news of worship. So the study on **the Church that Christ Built** began. As I made it through that first class, I realized there was more to learn on this subject. So I continued my study until I was asked to teach the adult class. The adult classroom has an overhead projection device that plugs into a computer. Since I often use PowerPoint at work, I decided to use PowerPoint and our overhead projector to teach the good news of Christ. Each week I would take my notes and convert them into classroom ready presentations. I travel quite a bit for my work, so many times I found myself finishing my lessons in airports and on airplanes. However, by the end of that quarter, I had converted my notes into a 12-week study on **the Church that Christ Built**. Teaching adults opened my eyes to a different level of questions than those I had been asked by the teens. So the study continued until I was asked to teach the young adult class. This time I refined my presentations and started writing down my thoughts and lessons as I presented the material. As I put my thoughts on paper, this book started to appear.

I did not set out to write a book, but somehow the idea to write this book would not go away. In fact, self-doubt, uncertainty of how to write, the fact that I'm not a good speller, what to write, how to publish, and what people would think all started to build up and nearly caused me to put the idea of writing a book to rest. However, God has a way of being bigger than our fears. I am not sure how God communicated with people in the Bible. In some cases He talked directly to them. In other cases people seemed to know what God wanted them to do. God never spoke to me, but I felt a push to write this book that can only be described as strange. I couldn't sleep because this book was on my mind and I felt guilty if I watched television instead of writing. Many times I would sit down at the computer at 10:00 or 11:00 at night and say, "OK already" and I would start to type. I am sure my sister Karla is glad that I am about done. She has always been good with English, so I asked her to be my editor. She agreed, but I am sure she has thought on more than one occasion, "Is English really his native language?" She has gone through several red ink pens, but her edits and suggestions have greatly improved the flow and content of this material.

Chapter Highlights

So here we are at the end of the book. I hope that this book has helped you realize that **The Church that Christ Built** is worth finding and that it is nothing less than awesome. However, to gain that insight, we had to go back to the basics. We had to go beyond preconceived notions. We had to question truths that once seemed so solid. We had to go back to the Bible, and that is where this book starts.

Chapters 1 – 3: Clearing the Way

The first three chapters focused on what truth is and how we define it. So many people think because something has been done a certain way for a long time, then that way must be correct. We found that a religion built from traditions and best intentions can be at risk. We studied two views concerning the silence of the Scriptures. One view suggests that silence is permissive while the other view suggests that silence is prohibitive. We found that when we go beyond the written and confirmed word of God, we are moving in an area that has no support. That is not to say that the Bible is outdated, boring, or even old-fashioned. We just believe that if God said it, we should do it. Our discussion on Biblical boundaries led to the CENI method of Bible study. This method uses commands, examples, and necessary inferences related to Biblical interpretations today. Basically, this method says that everything we do today must be tied back to Scripture in some way. Otherwise, we are building a faith on conjecture rather than the written word of God.

> Jeremiah 6:16 This is what the Lord says: "Stand at the crossroads and look; ask for the ancient paths, ask where the good way is, and walk in it, and you will find rest for your souls."

Chapters 4 - 5: God's Worship Plans

Once we established a way to study the Bible, we found that there are ways of worship that God approves as well as ways of worship that God does not. As we uncovered these truths, I found comfort in knowing I serve a God who actually thought enough of me to tell me what He likes. We don't have to guess, and we don't have to make things up. God is very clear on what He wants in worship. All we have to do is read the instructions.

Isaiah 58: 13-14 [13] "If you keep your feet from breaking the Sabbath and from doing as you please on my holy day, if you call the Sabbath a delight and the LORD's holy day honorable, and if you honor it by not going your own and not doing as you please or speaking idle words, [14] then you will find your joy in the LORD, and I will cause you to ride on the heights of the land and to feast on the inheritance of your father Jacob." The mouth of the LORD has spoken.

Chapters 6 – 8: The Early Church

The Church that Christ built did not just happen overnight. Christ did not think of the church as an afterthought. The apostles did not set up a club so they could visit once a week. We see Christ actively developing His church at least 600 years before the doors of the kingdom actually opened. We then see where He defines church as an assembly of people that represents the spiritual rocks in the walls of the kingdom. We read of the grand opening of Christ's church on the day of Pentecost with Peter giving the first sermon. We see the apostles are changed men. They are driven, they finally get what Christ was doing, and they become part of the foundation for the church as Christ intended. We see that the early Christians had a love and devotion for each other that we all need to work toward. Then at the stoning of Stephen, the bubble bursts. The Christians in Jerusalem were forced to flee, but when they found a place to stop, they could not keep quiet. The good news of Christ and the kingdom was too great to keep to themselves, so they started to set up churches everywhere. The attempt to snuff out this Christian movement actually fueled a movement that is still growing today.

2 Timothy 2:19 Nevertheless, God's solid foundation stands firm, sealed with this inscription: "The Lord knows those who are his," and, "Everyone who confesses the name of the Lord must turn away from wickedness."

Chapters 9 - 10: Church Organization

As the church was springing up all over the countryside, we see the development of the need for a formal organization of the church. Christ put this organization in place. The organization is subject to Christ who is the head of everything, but the members of the body are subject to the elders of a local congregation. There is no need for additional levels between the elders of a local congregation and Christ. Christ is still in charge. He is the one who has given some to be leaders of His body. However, we found that being a leader is not a passive job. It has a specific function. Leaders of the body of Christ are to prepare God's people for works of service so that they can reflect Christ.

Ephesians 4:11-13 [11]It was he (Christ) who gave some to be apostles, some to be prophets, some to be evangelists, and some to be pastors and teachers,

¹²to prepare God's people for works of service, so that the body of Christ may be built up ¹³until we reach unity in the faith and in the knowledge of the Son of God and become mature, attaining to the whole measure of the fullness of Christ.

Chapter 11: The Mission

All of these chapters lead us to the very point of **the Church that Christ Built**. Christ put in place a structure that would act as His body. This structure is to reflect the very nature of Christ Himself. When people look at the works of the church you attend, they should see the very essence of Christ Himself. Christ set up an organization that is to seek and save the lost by doing works of service. The combination of preaching, teaching, and caring worked for Christ. Christ walked on this earth for only 33 years and did not start His ministry until he was 30. However, He changed the world. Today, we can change the world if we can get back to doing what Christ set out for His body to do.

Ephesians 1:22-23 ²²And God placed all things under his feet and appointed him to be head over everything for the church, ²³which is his body, the fullness of him who fills everything in every way.

Wiring

It seems only fitting that an electrical engineer should close out the book with a story on wiring. Recently a friend of mine purchased a home. There was one problem that came up during the closing related to the basement wiring. It did not pass the inspection. Rather than try to get the previous owner to take care of the problem, we decided to fix it ourselves. When I walked into their new home, I was expecting to find a basement in bad shape. After all, if the wiring was messed up, I assumed the basement would be as well. However, to my surprise, the basement looked like a modern studio apartment with nicely painted walls, expensive carpet, full bathroom, and nice light fixtures mounted in a drop-down ceiling. Quite impressive until we started digging into the wiring. What a mess! Not only was the wiring not to code, it was dangerous. Wiring errors were causing lights to burn out, electronic equipment to fail, and, worst yet, the potential for electrical shock or even electrocution. We were amazed that someone could spend so much money on remodeling a basement but totally fell short with the wiring. We realized the previous owner did not intentionally jeopardize his investment. He just wired the basement the way he thought was best. Several hours were spent unraveling the problem. Finally we got it, but the experience taught me a lesson. Get the wiring right before the finish work is even started.

As I was moving ceiling tiles and pulling wire while trying not to mess up the nice walls, it dawned on me that the previous owner was not that much different than many in the religious community. Religions rarely, if ever, try to mislead people. In fact, religions are filled with people with good intentions. Many will spend fortunes making their building look spectacular yet not have the fundamentals of religion correctly in place.

When that home inspector looked at the wiring, he was not looking at what could be seen on the outside. His instruments allowed him to see what was on the inside. The fact that the exterior gave an impression of perfection did not sway the inspector's report. The wiring was wrong and his job was to alert the new homeowner of the problem. I am sure the previous owner was shocked to hear he had done a bad job on his basement. He may even have gotten upset and tried to have another inspection. The problem is that no matter how much the previous owner tried, the wiring was a safety hazard that did not pass code. If he had just spent a few hours in the library researching wiring, he would have avoided so many potentially damaging results.

Someday the ultimate inspector is going to grade us. If we live our life according to the code, we will be fine. If, however, we look good on the outside but are wired wrong on the inside, we may very well be in jeopardy of the worst kind of shock. If only we would spend time reading the instruction manual, ask questions, and make sure that our religious practices are consistent with what our Lord wants, then many of today's religious problems would be avoided.

The Church that Christ Built strives to follow the commands and examples laid out for us in Scripture. This book attempts to describe them in a way that shows the true beauty of this perfect, God-given structure. We cannot improve on perfection, but we can mess perfection up.

Cities of Refuge

At the start of this book, I did not want to bias anyone by mentioning the congregation where I attend, but rather research **The Church that Christ Built** strictly from the perspective given to us in scripture. In so doing, we can all evaluate our religious practices and make adjustments as needed to stay in line with what Christ actually did build. However, there are so many religious groups and titles of churches in the world today, finding a church can be very difficult. As a result, here is what I look for when selecting a church.

I have had the opportunity to travel to every continent but Antarctica. During my travels, I try to find a religious organization to visit. When searching for a church, I am often reminded of the cities of refuge that are described in the book of Numbers. A city of refuge (Numbers 35) was set aside for people that had accidently killed someone. That person would escape to these cities for safety. The part about accidently killing someone is not what I am referencing, but rather the searching for a safe haven. Imagine running for your life, seeing the walls of the city in the distance, and hoping you could make it to the city in time to be safe from harm's way. When I am on the road, the need to find a church to attend is as important to me as it would have been to those in the Old Testament trying to find a city of refuge. Inside these cities, you would have been safe, they would have known the rules, they would have been helpful and encouraging, and they would have taken care of you. These are exactly the traits I look for in a church when I am at home or on the road. **The Church that Christ Built**, when found, means that I am safe, edified, encouraged, uplifted, and recharged to continue on my journey.

One challenge in finding a church is to realize that the name on the building can have very little to do with what goes on in the building. This is an unfortunate result of Satan being alive and active in the world today. He is the master of confusion and if he can convince us of being saved strictly with our religious affiliation, then we are in trouble.

The Bible is not silent on providing us with a starting point with regards to looking for His Church. In scripture we can find several titles of religious groups who follow the pattern of **the Church that Christ Built.** One such title was applied to the churches in the book of Romans.

> Romans 16:16 Greet one another with a holy kiss. All the **churches of Christ** send greetings.

Starting with the name of a religious organization that can be tracked to scripture is a good place to begin your search. The Church of Christ strives to be a Bible based and Bible guided fellowship of believers. We try very hard to please the Lord and to only speak were the Bible speaks and remain silent where it is silent. However, please keep in mind that no matter where we attend, we must do our due diligence to ensure we are acceptably following the pattern of worship given to us by the Lord. Let us recognize the difference between saying "we are a Christian because we worship" and "we worship because we are a Christian". Make the latter phrase our goal and always keep Christ in focus. Then we will not deviate from **the Church that Christ Built**.

Christ will make sure those that look for Him will find Him!

The Touch of the Master's Hand

Subtle Changes

The Church that Christ built has now been in existence for nearly 2,000 years. However, if we are not careful, it only takes a little change each year to completely lose track of what Christ gave us. To illustrate, did you happen to notice the boxes on the right side of each chapter's page one? Those boxes were being filled in as we progressed through the book? If not, take a minute to flip through the pages of the book. You will see the boxes filling in as the book comes to an end. This filling in of the boxes is an example of how subtle changes can happen without anyone thinking there is a problem. If each box represents a year, then nearly 50 years of change just happened. Those boxes are about the size of a box that would allow 2,000 of them to fit on this page. If only a small change were made each year, we would hardly notice it in our lifetime. However, let those changes go on for 2,000 years, and the original intent of Christ's church would be lost. Fortunately, we have the Bible and with that we can always get back to Christ's perfect design.

Chief Cornerstone

As we come to the close of this journey, I can't help but think of the following poem by Myra Brooks Welch.

"Twas battered and scarred, and the auctioneer thought it scarcely worth his while to waste much time on the old violin, but held it up with a smile. "What am I bidden, good folks," he cried, "Who'll start the bidding for me?" "A dollar, a dollar," then, two! Only two? "Two dollars, and who'll make it three? "Three dollars, once; three dollars, twice; Going for three . . ." But no, from the room, far back, a grey-haired man came forward and picked up the bow; Then, wiping the dust from the old violin, and tightening the loose strings, He played a melody pure and sweet as a caroling angel sings.

The music ceased, and the auctioneer, with a voice that was quiet and low, said: "What am I bid for the old violin?" And he held it up with the bow. "A thousand dollars, and who'll make it two? "Two thousand! And who'll make it three? "Three thousand, once; three thousand, twice; and going and gone." said he.

The people cheered, but some of them cried, "We do not quite understand What changed its worth?" Swift came the reply: "The touch of a master's hand."

Jesus was the stone that the builders tossed aside. However, the stone the builders rejected became the chief cornerstone of a mighty structure that has stood for over 2,000 years. Christ did not build a building with bricks and mortar. He built a spiritual building made with living stones, Christians.

1 Peter 2:5 you also, like living stones, are being built into a spiritual house to be a holy priesthood, offering spiritual sacrifices acceptable to God through Jesus Christ.

As we reflect on this book, it becomes apparent that **the Church that Christ built** was truly touched by the ultimate Master's hand.

Questions to Consider

1. Find at least 5 names of religious groups mentioned in the New Testament that adhere to the Church that Christ Built.
2. In John, chapter 10: 1-21, what does it mean to know the voice of the shepherd?
3. A sheep will not listen to a stranger's voice. What will the sheep do when they do not recognize his voice?
4. Read Ezekiel 34 and Jeremiah 23 and describe what makes a bad Shepherd and what will the Lord do for his scattered sheep?

Bibliography

I have collected information on **the Church that Christ built** for several years. Much of my research came from notes I have taken from Bible classes, books, the Internet, but primarily the Bible. The following books and web sites were particularly useful:

Reference Books

Blake, William. An Almanac of the Christian Church. Minneapolis, Minnesota: Bethany House Publishers, 1987, ISBN: 0-87123-897-7.

Cloer, Eddie. What is "The Church?" - Identifying the Nature and Design of the New Testament Church. Searcy, AR: Resource Publications, 1993, ISBN 0-945441-16-9.

Echols, Eldred. The Most Excellent Way: Overcoming Chronic Issues That Divide the Church, Fort Worth, Texas: Sweet Publishing, 1994, ISBN: 0-8344-0233-5.

Ferguson, Everett. The New Testament Church, Abilene, Texas: Biblical Research Press, 1968, ISBN 0-89112-108-0.

Hook, Cecil, Free to Speak, Beaverton, OR: Publishing Ministry, 1986.

Howard, Alton. Songs of Faith and Praise, West Monroe, LA: Howard Publishing Co., Inc. 1998, ISBN 1-878990-34-9.

Howard, V. E. What is the Church of Christ?, West Monroe, Louisiana: Central Printers and Publishers, 1971.

Mead, Frank, Handbook of Denominations in the United States, Nashville, TN: Abingdon Press, 1990, ISBN: 0-687-16572-5.

Web Sites

http://www.biblegateway.com/, Bible scripture search program.
http://www.ccel.org/contrib/exec_outlines/home.htm, Church information maintained by Copeland, Mark.
http://www.padfield.com/, Church information maintained by David Padfield.
http://www.beavertonchurchofchrist.net, Church information maintained by Mark Dunagan.
http://www.studylight.org/, Study Light Bible Dictionary.
http://www.barbados.org/poetry/masters.htm, Source for "The Touch of the Master's Hand" poem.

The Church that Christ built book is well suited for a 12-week study program. The book consists of 12 chapters, one for each week, with discussion questions at the end of each chapter. The course has been taught to many different groups including:

- Teens
- Young Adults
- Adults
- Small Groups
- Home Groups

Over 2,000 years ago, the King's treasure was made available to all. Many that accepted the gift found it of such value that they gave their life to protect it.

Today, the King's treasure is still available, but has 2,000 years blurred its' splendor and beauty?

In this book we will wipe away the years of dust and debris to uncover the original splendor and glory of the King's treasure.

The King's treasure is **the Church that Christ built**. The brilliance of our King can be seen more clearly when the framework of His Church is examined.

About the author
Kevin has been a member of the Church for over 30 years. He has taught Bible lessons, developed Church curriculum, and recruited Bible school teachers. Although Kevin is active in his local Church, he supports his family as an Electrical Engineer. He graduated from Ohio University in Athens, Ohio in 1986 with a Bachelor of Science in Electrical Engineering and he received his Masters in Electrical Engineering from Ohio State University in Columbus, Ohio in 2000. He has worked in industrial automation for over 20 years and has had the opportunity of travel around the world on several occasions. In addition to his Church and engineering responsibilities, he is a husband and a father. Kevin has been married to his college sweetheart Kim for over 25 years and they have three fine Christian children Kayla, Kameron, and Colten.

Made in the USA
Coppell, TX
21 May 2021

56120373R00098